Colts
Student Voices:
Poems, Stories, and Essays

The Students of Carson High School

Published and Distributed:
Milligan Books, Inc.

Cover Design: Kevin Allen

Formatting: Milligan Books

First Printing, October 2009
10987654321
ISBN 978-0-9824292-6-6
Publisher's Note:

Milligan Books, Inc.
1425 W. Manchester Ave., Suite C
Los Angeles, California 90047
Website: www.milliganbooks.com
Telephone: (323) 750-3592

Colts

Student Voices:
Poems, Stories, and Essays

The Students of Carson High School

MILLIGAN BOOKS, INC.　　　　　　　　CALIFORNIA

Acknowledgements

COLTS
Poems, stories and essays by the freshmen students of the class of 2012
Carson Senior High School
Carson, California
Kenneth Keener, Principal

⚜

LAUSD Local District 8
Linda Del Cueto, Superintendent
Dr. Dona Stevens, Administrator of Instruction

⚜

Los Angeles Unified School District
Ramon Cortines, Superintendent

⚜

Published with the financial support of
GEAR UP
(Gaining Early Awareness and Readiness for Undergraduate Programs),
a federally funded program in Local District 8 of LAUSD
Carol Takemoto, Director

FOREWORD

Producing a literate population has always been one of the most important purposes of the public school system. Often literacy is measured in terms of standardized tests, but the ability to write creatively is a more authentic measure of literacy. By this measure these students of Carson High School pass with high marks.

This anthology contains poems and stories from about a hundred students, mostly freshmen, from Carson High School in Carson, California. Carson is an urban high school, part of the huge Los Angeles school system. It reflects all of the diversity of our modern American cities, and Carson students experience all of the problems faced by youth in America today.

The students wrote these poems and stories, but that wouldn't have happened without the active support of their teachers. They also get credit for this book.

The main financial support for this publication came from GEAR UP (Gaining Early Awareness and Readiness for Undergraduate Programs), a federal grant program in LAUSD's Local District 8 designed to increase student participation in advanced education after high school. GEAR UP will follow these students from 6th grade in the nearby middle schools through their senior year at Carson. GEAR UP provides a wide range of resources and activities to promote student participation in higher education, including peer mentoring, motivational speakers, college field trips, summer academic enrichment programs, in-class college tutors, professional development for teachers, and parent training.

We hope that this book will be an inspiration to these students and all of their classmates at Carson High to think of themselves as writers, now and always. Whether it's a business letter or a poem, a resume or a story, writing well is one of the keys to success in life.

Congratulations to all of these young writers!!

Jeff Horton
GEAR UP Tutor Coordinator
August 13, 2009

TABLE OF CONTENTS

Academy of Cultural and Ethnic Studies (ACES)

Lead Teacher: Ms. Simmons
Participating Teachers: Ms. Dev
Ms. Kolar

This is Just to Say
By Victor Tenorio

I have eaten the chewy cookies
Stored in the ceramic jar
On the top shelf

Which were
Supposed to be saved for the
party

Forgive me
They were so melty-soft and chocolaty

∞

My Leather Recliner
By Treshawn Carter

So much depends on

my leather recliner

When I lay on it, I fall into a deep, pleasant sleep

it has a green, velour pillow and a red ribbed throw

just calling my name saying, "Come sleep on me!"

My Life

By Jovanny Tovar

I was noisy and cried all the time
With soft skin and damp diapers
Luminous eyes and an adorable smile
Just an insignificant little bundle
People cooed intently over my sweet laughter
While my gestures remained remarkably ominous

I grew tall and talkative
With an abundant amount
Of knowledge to behold
With a query in my future
and luxurious treasures in my path
My eyes sparkle with content

I will be a long-lost memory
In the wind
Just another wish ungranted and miscounted
Set free from life's discontent and misery
My voice silenced by the suffering sight of my love

A Whirlwind

By Jackie Castillo

My life was a whirlwind of emotions
I was moved in many ways
Daddy's little girl
Is what they called me
I was the ocean breeze
Stuck in a cave

My life is a war
Taking different risks wherever I can
I am a bard
My love for music and my experiences
I am an ocean of emotions

My life will be a summer morning
The sun shining on the dew of opportunity
The heat of choices surrounding me
A never-ending wind of obstacles
The horizon of life will now set

Changes

By Daniela Martinez

I was a little trouble maker
Happy but crazy
Loud and giggly
Funny and caring and sometimes slow

My life is full of energy
I'm funny, hyper, and outgoing
It's rare to see me down since I'm always smiling
I'll hear you out when you need somebody
I make a lot of mistakes like everybody

I will mature
Become a careful and responsible person
More likely a calm, intelligent, motherly person
Try to accomplish my goals and graduate
I will cautiously learn from good and bad

HER: PAST, PRESENT, AND FUTURE

By Seanette Fualau

Back in the day when I was a kid
Was the most fun time of my life
Didn't have to worry about anything
Raised by the best people
Who taught me right from wrong
The past is the past
And right now, we are in the present

Life's not going too well
Lost many loved ones
Trying to do my best and not mess up
Trying to make my parents proud
This is the present, now let's go to my future

I'm a successful person
Proved so many wrong
Bought my mom a Jaguar
My hard work has paid off
Now I am who I said I would be

LIFE

By James Toomalatai

My father's watchful eye, my mother's greeting smile
My brother, big and strong, my sister, singing songs
I am a child, a baby
Just waiting for my growth to begin to unfold
Waiting as time begins to slip by
Always wishing to listen to my mother's lullabies one more time

I am 14 going on 15
As time moves by, these are the days in which my dreams begin to
take flight
Working, training, trying to do what's right
Making mistakes, hiding the tears I cry
My parents' clutch begins to loosen more and more
Now there is freedom, which I hadn't seen before

My sun has set over a clear horizon
As one life finishes, another begins
I wish to see the world one last time
My eyes close on this story of mine

A Metaphor

By Salvador Ibarra

My life was a shadow
Hiding from the presence of the sun
Willing to show myself to those who seek
I was the wind only willing to whisper
I was the winter waiting for the warmth of the sun

My life is a torrent of obstacles
Now emotions everywhere
I am an impenetrable shield
Protecting myself from the wrath of drugs
Fighting the winds of negativity

My life will be like winter
Unexpected storms happening
Opportunity snowing down on me
Then the flower will bloom
And the sun will melt the snow away

Me Now

By Markeace Gill

I was a bad boy and a member of a crew, doing dumb things and nearly killing someone.

I remember when my great grandmother passed away.

I heard that my grandfather and my uncle fight for my first time.

I saw my friend on the ground crying because of the pain from getting shoot.

I worried that I would end up dead because of my neighborhood.

I thought I was headed for jail because of the people I hung out with.

But, I want to change.

I am a nice person who really put my mom through hell, but now I'm different.

I think that people think of you from the outside, not the inside.

I need to fulfill a goal—that I could be making millions of dollars a day.

I try to hang out with intelligent classmates.

I feel like I want to just cry when I think of the pain in my heart.

I forgive but I don't forgive my uncle being shot seven times.

Now I can change.

I have been staying away from gang members and everything has changed.

I choose to start working out to get some meat on my little bones.

I dream that I will become the richest person in the world, not just the United States.

I hope that I can become a very, very powerful man.

I predict that I can be anything I put my mind to.

I know that I will be buff, tall, rich, powerful, and *the next Black president.*

I will change

Ma Life

By Kenneth Savage

I'm little and flashy
And itz all 'bout me
I'm a young buck, killen 'em nasty
I'm a mean, lean, money-makin' machine
So you know whassup already
I be on the block, right?
Lyricz buzzin' in my right mind
Just a young brotha hustlin to get right
Who they call you?
They call me Young Bubz
Ain't born wit a silver spoon
But a child of the ghetto
Raised wit a different tune

My Life: Past, Present, and Future

By Fransisco Corona

I was afraid
There were a lot of drive-bys
I was scared of getting shot
Many times, I had to fight back

I moved from Watts to Carson
Here, my house isn't shot at
It's different from over there
And I feel lucky
To be out of danger

I don't want to mess up like before
I want to graduate from college
I want to be a policeman
I want to be somebody

WESTSIDE STORY

BY JESSE TORRES

I was a legend...
I had it all waving in the wind
I was a crazy rascal
Sitting in the car-seat looking at my feet

My life is a rollercoaster
Can't get off till it stops
Grades are what I need to succeed
I am a tall tree, deep in the country
When I am in the moment
My life is crazy with no place to run

I will soon be a lonely wolf, hunting for his prey
I'll be blinded by the light,
Old and grey
Watching the days fade away
While my hair turns grey, I will watch my kids play,
Will be the day I tilt away

I am a river

By Brandon Brown

In the daytime, I'm going and going
In the nighttime, I'm overflowing
If you wish to see me
You will notice that I am headed towards my own destiny

I am the weather
No one knows the real me
Nor can predict what I will do next
In reality
I shall always remain a mystery

I am a wolf
The leader of the tribe
What I say always goes
There is no refusing
There is no, "No."

I am a mermaid from the sea

By Marlen Castro

I wonder how life will turn out to be
I hear waves and whales
I see water and seaweed
I want a dolphin to play with me
I am a mermaid from the sea

I pretend to swim under the sea
I feel jittery and sweet
I touch a silver fishie
I worry about how life will turn out to be
I cry when something isn't for me
I am a mermaid from the sea

I understand mermaids are happy
I say love is what we need
I dream of me and you being silly
I try having fun under the sea
I hope the sea will be a good home for me
I am a mermaid from the sea

I AM A VERY INTELLIGENT AND GIFTED YOUNG LADY

By Jevonne Fisher

I wonder if I will graduate from high school in 2012
I hear whispering sounds
I see a door to success
I want to become a lawyer
I am a very intelligent and gifted young lady

I pretend to be a lawyer
I feel like I can fly
I touch the clouds
I worry about violence
I cry about the deaths of teenagers
I am a very intelligent and gifted young lady

I understand that life isn't easy
I say that anything is possible
I dream of owning my own law firm
I try to stay away from negative energy
I hope that I achieve all my goals and dreams
I am a very intelligent and gifted young lady

I am the special guy in that girl's life

By Jason Duproza

I wonder if I'm on her mind
I hear her whispering in my ear
I see her waving her hand as she leaves
I want to know if our eyes will meet again

I am the special guy in that girl's life
I understand that we are apart
I remember saying things I didn't mean
I dream of her holding me tight
I try not to forget what we had
I hope that one day, my love will reunite us
I am that girl's ex

I AM JUST A BOY IN A CROWD

By Anthony Devoe

I wonder if she'll pick me
I hear her cheerful laugh
I see her sweet smile
I want her undying love
I am just a boy in a crowd

I am just a boy in a crowd
I know that truly understand her
I say that I love her
I dream dreams about her
I try to talk to her
I hope that we will be together someday soon
I am just a boy in a crowd

I am sports-minded

By Myles Young

I wonder if I can make it to the NFL
I hear helmets and pads hitting each other
I see myself sticking Desean Jackson
I want to play against the best
I am a football player

I am sports-minded
I pretend to be taller
I feel the best when I'm running on the grass
I worry a lot about getting hurt
I cry when I drop the game's winning touchdown
I am a football player

I am sports-minded
I understand even though I am not the biggest person,
I still have the best game
I say that this is C-House
I dream of being in the Hall of Fame
I hope that I can make it to the NFL
I am a football player

I am a wolf

By Jennifer Carrillo

I love to run in the woods and smell the flowers
While I hunt around for dinner
I sleep all night and day while hoping my dreams come true
I play with my family and train them to hunt
I look at the sky and see the stars
I play in the rain and have lots of fun
Lastly, I howl at night to connect with other wolves

I am an orange tree

By Christopher Baltazar

The wind blows and hits my leaves
The wind blowing is my relaxed attitude
The leaves falling is how calm I am
The tree moving softly is the patience that I have for people
When I am watered, it is like taking a quick swim
When people pick my oranges
I feel angry
But when birds come nest in my branches
And make their new homes
All the happiness that I have is revealed

Yellow Rose of Maria

By Maria Correa

I see the flower blooming beneath the sail
The sound of the blooming flower is as quiet as a mouse
It tastes like a milkshake running down your throat
It is as bright as a yellow orange and tastes like a
Stick of freshly made butter

Too many problems

By Erisa Joy Catipon

I felt like dying
With one call through my phone
The problems began

Broken-hearted
She never stopped crying
Saying that she no longer wants to live
She always says sorry
But it's not working anymore
Like a car stopped in the middle of the road
Trying to keep on going even without gas

∞

By Crystal Dilworth

As my room warmed my heart
And filled me with comfort and simplicity
The tears streamed down my face
Quickly hitting an old car and rusty shopping carts,
The rain raced and raced
As I looked out the window, I heard the rain sing to me
Beating the ground like a hollow drum

Who Is Mabel?

By Erisa Joy Catipon

At noon, Mabel emerged
She was a woman whose beauty had
Blown away like leaves falling apart
She used to be a glamorous, long-legged woman
But now she is just an old woman
Sitting in a worn-out wheelchair
Drinking some stale brown coffee
Out of a sad little coffee mug
Her once-beautiful face was lined and wrinkled,
Looking like a brown paper bag that had been crumpled
A million times and then thrown in the trash
The beauty that was once there is now just a memory

∞

By Natalie Martin

At noon, Mabel came out the back door
She was old with little legs
Her lips were so chapped, they looked like they were growing mold
Her eyes were red and bloody looking
Her gray hair was falling out
Everyone was scared of Mabel

Don't Sit On the Baby!

By Tramaine Harris

In 1995, my brother was seven years old and I was one. His favorite show to watch was WWE, which featured his favorite wrestler, Yokosuna. He asked me if I knew who that certain wrestler was and of course, since I was only one, I said no. He said, "Say it after me. Yo—ko—SU—na!"

"Yokossss..." I babbled in a baby voice. My mispronounced version of his favorite wrestler made him mad. He kept trying to correct my pronunciation but I kept repeating, "Yokossss...."

"Say the wrong name again!" he yelled, "And I am going to turn the TV volume way up!" He knew that the loud noise would scare me. So, of course I started to cry and he said "Shut up!" quietly, but violently. He didn't want my mother and father to come see what we were doing. Since I kept crying and didn't shut up like he wanted me to, he tried sitting on me to make me stop. I kept crying louder and louder, both from the loud noise as well as from being sat on.

I don't actually remember my parents actually coming in and seeing him sitting on top of me, but I can definitely imagine their horrified expressions. My brother got a whooping for a long time, which resulted in him having to think twice before he ever sat on me again. As my brother was crying an immense waterfall of tears while getting whipped, I smiled sneakily. My parents said loudly, "Will you do this again?"

"NO!" he yelled.

"Go to your room and think about what you did!" they said. At that, my brother ran to his room and slammed the door shut. After sitting on me, my parents did not allow my brother to watch TV for three weeks. I forgot what day they told him that, but either way, it was a super three weeks because I had the TV all to myself. To make things even better, my mom fed me my favorite food at the time, applesauce, and gave me my favorite drink, apple juice.

A couple of days later, my brother and I started getting along. My pit bull had just given birth to puppies and we began to play with the puppies together and watch them fall asleep on our laps. Today he is twenty years old while I am fourteen, and I look up to him as my role model. A lot of things have changed since that time that he tried to shut me up by sitting on me. However, the thing that has remained the same is that we both enjoy hearing this story again and again, and making others laugh with it.

A "True" Friend Can Be Your Enemy

By Ashley Benavidez

The sun shone in my face during fourth period P.E. I was with my best friend, Melanie. We were walking our last lap around the field of Stephen M. White Middle School and arguing about the boy she had been dating for almost ten months. I told her, "He doesn't deserve you. You're like his pet. He calls you whenever he wants and plus he you know that he's cheating on you."

She said, "Ashley, you're supposed to be my friend and right now you're acting stupid and jealous."

I started to laugh. "Ha ha! Jealous? That's dumb, why would I be jealous of a dumb, worthless relationship?"

She replied, "Whatever, its not like I care about what you think anyway," made a face, and ran ahead of me to finish the lap. I was really mad because she didn't want to listen to anything I had to say. I tried talking to her again during sixth period. She said, "Why are you even talking to me? I don't talk to fake friends!"

I was really angry when she told me that. I was her friend for life and she knew it. "Whatever!" I said loudly. "At least I'm not the stupid one who allows myself to be treated like trash!" We continued arguing while class was in session until the teacher stopped us. Since that day, she would always insult me when I passed by her yelling, "FAKE!" giving me dirty looks, and telling the rest of her friends to do the same.

Every time that happened, I felt terrible. I had flashbacks of when we were close friends, and started wondering how we grew apart. We'd been best friends since the third grade and she was like a sister to me. We had our inside jokes, goofy walks, our own dances, etc. We would do everything together and tell each other everything. I thought that it was unfortunate that we'd stopped being friends just because of one unfaithful boy. I wish she'd never been blinded by a love that didn't correspond to her, and I felt awful being ditched just because of a stupid boy.

Today I have another best friend, Stephanie, who I met in the eight grade. She is a great friend too, but I still don't really know her like I knew Melanie. Melanie and I were not alike internally. I would do my nails, make-up, hair, and look very cute, while she dressed very casually. She only did her make-up once in a while and never did her nails. She was way more of a tomboy than I was, but that didn't matter to me. It mattered that she was caring (too much sometimes,) and had a big heart. We had a necklace that said "Best Friends." She wore the part that said "friends" and I had the part that said "best."

A while has passed, but we still have not talked. I go to Carson High, while she goes to Lakewood. I would like to talk to her and catch up, but I still feel something wouldn't even allow me to say "Hi!" because she has said and done so many things to hurt my feelings.

Best friends can come and go but some stay. The ones that are loyal to you and stay around through both good and bad times are like your family members. Melanie and I used to be like this, but no more. I hope that one day, we can put our pride aside and become friends again, because I think about her and the good times we shared more often than I'd like to admit.

Hoop Dreams

By Armon Mathis

Until the time I was 12, I played basketball for Rogers Park League and the Gardena and Inglewood YMCA, but I'd never played for a traveling basketball team before. I loved playing basketball for these organizations because it was really fun to meet new people and learn new techniques. Both the park league and the Y taught me not to be scared of or back off from any battle on the court. Lastly, I made many friends and always had a great time.

About halfway through 2006, I joined my first traveling basketball team, the Long Beach Sixers. I had heard about them from my mother, who had learned of them through a co-worker whose son played for the older Sixers team. After a few practices, I became good friends with my teammates, Justin and Roman. Justin had just moved to the Sixers from another team, the Gymrats, and like me, this was Roman's first year of traveling basketball.

When Justin, Roman, and I went to sign up for the Sixers, I was really excited when our coach told us that the team was going to San Diego for a tournament. We met at the LB Jordan gym, where we held practice. The next day, we left around 10 am, and Justin was really psyched when he found out that we were playing his old team, the Gymrats. When we got to the hotel in San Diego, I automatically told my mother that everyone was meeting at Roman's house for the first night to "kick it," and meet each other. That night was a blast! We swam in the pool, snacked all night, and of course, chatted up the ladies.

When it was time to play the games, we were on a winning streak. Justin told us that the Gymrats had great skills and would be difficult to beat. Even so, we still hung with them neck in neck all the way until the end when they ended up winning the game by two points. We were really mad and disappointed, but we survived. The next day, we had two more games and meritoriously won both. We took second place with lots of praise and gigantic smiles on our faces. Upon returning home, we practiced the next day and for the entire rest of the week. After that, we didn't play for about two weeks so the new members could practice their plays. Following our two-week break, we played games for three weeks straight with some wins and some losses, but mostly wins.

When we played a game at Lynwood High about three months later, we met up with the Gymrats again. They came out strong and fast but so did we. Again, we were neck in neck, but this time we won. However, Justin, Roman, and I had been watching the Gymrats closely and it seemed that we clicked with their "style" more than that of the Sixers. In addition, we had heard that when it came to recruitment, the Gymrats got way more exposure than the Sixers. We all wanted to play varsity basketball in high school, so we decided that moving to the Gymrats was the right thing to do. So after the game, Roman's step dad approached the coach and talked to him about the three of us playing for the Gymrats. He completely went for it, and told us to meet him at Wilson Park at six pm on Thursday.

As Roman and I watched them play, we knew that we were ready to make the switch. Justin, who had already played with the Gymrats, already knew the deal. After practice, we had a meeting with the coach. He asked us about our determination and our love for the sport. We gave him our answer and the following week, we had our first practice. It was a serious workout and there was no time for playing around. That day, I also learned how much I weighed and how to maneuver my body correctly. After practice, the coach asked us to reflect on our experience and of course we had nothing but good things to say. After we started playing with the Gymrats full-time, we clicked really well with the Gymrats family. Our teammates were really supportive and the coaches really liked us. I loved every single moment of playing with the Gymrats.

The next year (2007-2008) was my second year with the Gymrats. I felt more confident because I knew everybody and they all really liked my friends and me. We decided to meet up with my old coach to express to him that there were no hard feelings and to let him know that the only reason we left was to be able to have more opportunities. After talking to the coach, we talked amongst ourselves and compared our leaving the Sixers to join the Gymrats, to Shaq leaving the Lakers for the Heat and then the Suns.

After about a month, the Gymrats coach told us, "When you boys put on that red, white, and blue Gymrats uniform, you become a man. You are playing a sport you love, so put your all into it." Little did I know that around this time, Carson, Long Beach Poly, Compton and LB Jordan High Schools were all watching the way that my friends and I played, and wanted to offer us a starting position on their varsity basketball team.

This event has affected me significantly because now I have a position of great importance—a starting position on Carson High School's basketball team. At this rate, my goal is to have a scholarship by next year. I will continue my hard work both on and off the court in order to fulfill my goal and be as successful as possible.

Missing Papa

By Jessica Alvarez

When I was younger--probably around six years old—I was really close to my father. My father and I were like two magnets stuck together. I loved him very much and I also felt like he loved me. Unfortunately, due to certain circumstances in life, my mother separated us and I never saw him again.

My father's name is Jaime Alvarez. He was born in San Francisco and so was I. Before moving to Wilmington, I used to live in San Francisco. The apartment where I lived was located in Palo Alto, near Stanford University. I lived in San Francisco from the time I was born all the way to when I was about three years old. At that time, I was an only child and I felt like both a mommy's and a daddy's girl. Although I really loved my mom, I still always felt closer to my dad.

When I was younger I did not have that much stuff, but my dad still tried to make me happy, no matter what. I saw my dad as a role model. While other little girls my age played with their Barbie dolls and other toys, I felt that with my dad at my side I did not need any material items. My father and I always did plenty of activities such as visit the beach everyday, go to San Fran's Chinatown for walks, and eat Chinese food. We would also would go swimming and visit my grandparents all the time. The thing that I liked doing the most with him was going to Pier 39. We would get on a tiny boat that took us to Angel Island, a beautiful little island where we used to go for walks and eat. I enjoyed everything I did with him, but one special memory that I will always have in my heart is when we would go crab catching at Baker Beach. I loved doing that with him. When we returned home we'd cook and eat them. While we cooked the crabs, our mouths watered. We would eat them with salt and lemon or with a special butter that tasted like popcorn. As an appetizer, we would make rice and beans, which also fragrant and tasted very delicious.

I thought everything was going perfectly. I was the happiest girl in the world until one day it started feeling like I was living in a bad dream that I thought would never end. What happened was that my mom and dad decided to get divorced and take separate paths in life. My mom left San Francisco and took me with her. When this happened, I felt horrible. I still saw my dad during Thanksgiving vacation and summer vacation. At first, he used to call me all the time and ask, "Are you coming to see me soon?"

"Yes," I'd scream, and jump with joy.

Although I did not live with my dad, I was always happy to at least go see him during vacation. That was what had kept me going since I left San Francisco, heartbroken. As years passed, I was still visiting my dad. He would also call me since my mom never let me call him. We kept doing our favorite activities and I never got bored. Therefore, I thought leaving San Francisco and my dad was the worst thing that could happen to me. It turned out I was wrong.

One summer, when I was about six years old, I went to San Francisco and I saw my dad. I told him I was scared of having so much fun, because what if the fun couldn't last forever? I told him I never wanted us to be apart. He responded that he would never let that happen and he would always keep us together. Summer ended and I went back home with my mom in Wilmington.

After that summer, my mom got mad at him and told me that I was never allowed to see him again. He also stopped calling me, most probably due to something my mother had said to him to get him to leave me alone. I made a effort to find out his number, but I wasn't successful. Not being able to see him tore up my heart and my happiness. My life was never the same.

As this point in my life, I was always lonely and never seemed to have any fun. Even though my mom was always with me, I still felt like I needed my dad since he was the parent that I was more comfortable with. Since then, time has passed and things have gotten better. About two years ago, I let all my anger and sadness go, and have tried my best to be happy. I don't know exactly what my mom told him and why he had to abandon me just like that. Even though that destroyed me, I forgave him a long time ago.

This Thanksgiving, a miracle occurred. My aunt and I were talking in her room when suddenly, my cousin Flaviano came in and asked my aunt if she wanted to talk to Uncle Jim. My heart started pounding really hard because I had a feeling that "Uncle Jim," might be my dad, Jaime. It turned out that I was correct. I was so shocked, I felt like fainting. She asked me if I wanted to talk to him and I replied, "Of course!" My dad and I started talking and he said he was doing fine. I felt really weird because a lot of years had passed and I know that he knew that he was no longer talking to a little girl, but a young woman. Right before we hung up, he gave me his cell phone number and I gave him mine. But he never calls me even though I called him.

At this point in my life, it seems as if the story is repeating itself. I told my mom that I had his phone number and she wasn't very happy about that. She does not let me call him anymore. The absence of my dad makes me sad, but it does not affect my actions that much anymore. I try to keep a positive attitude about life and keep going. I definitely plan on seeing my dad again. I will wait until I am eighteen and go look for him so I can see him at least one more time.

ALONE IN THE WORLD

By Claudia Barajas

Alone in the world. This is how I feel when my mother moves to the United States. I am two years old when my mother leaves me. I am being raised by my grandparents and my fifteen uncles and aunts. As time passes, I keep on praying to God for my mommy to come back. I am still little and have just started to understand the world. I am having a really tough time without a mom or a dad to tell me, "Don't do this because you can get hurt." At this point, I have been growing up with mostly men around so I don't have anyone to teach me how to be a girl. My aunts have been in and out of the house and I really don't tell them what's going on or how I feel bad because I have a one year old little sister who really needs me. My grandpa says he's okay, but I can see in his eyes that he's tired. The food we eat is not good. In fact, I barely even eat because we're so poor. But my heart is rich with longing—especially for a mother or father.

Many people can't tell what I go through. Now I'm twelve years old and I live with my aunt. My little sister always asks me, "Where is my mother?" not meaning my mom, but my grandmother. She's never met my mom or my dad. We were living in a strange land, where I feared for my live and for my little sister's life but now we live in Mexicali and have a better life. I have been in Mexicali for two weeks. I'm starting school tomorrow and I'm scared. My mother calls and tells us we will meet her in two years. I don't remember her face but I feel her love. My sister does not feel it because she hasn't seen her since she was a baby. Lately she is depressed and tells me that she wants my grandmother and doesn't want go with her real mother. I understand how she feels, after all our mother is a stranger to her.

Two years pass and we finally get to meet her. She looks very weird and foreign and says, "I love you, my child." I enter the United States and see a small child at our house. "Who is that?" I ask.

She answers, "This is your little brother, Robert John, and this is my husband, your stepfather, Robert Mojica.

"Another father?" I ask. "How does that work?"

"What do you mean?" my mom answers.

"How can you be married to two men?" I question her. This is when she tells me that my real father left her and never loved her. What she told me breaks my heart and that night right before bedtime, I ask God how my father could have forgotten about me, his own child, and wonder if I would see him again.

Now I'm 17 years old and I still feel lonely and not completely like myself. I know that a lot of other teens my age have gone through something similar which has affected them. My struggle has affected me in both good and bad ways. The good way is that now I have a better life and if I keep on studying I can be successful and have a good career and become a better person. The bad way in which this incident has affected me is that I don't always my mom or my stepdad and feel that my real father is nothing but a cold stranger. Most of the time, I don't really feel that my mom is part of my family, but just a great friend. Hopefully one day, I can pick up the missing pieces of my "life puzzle" and glue them back together in the right way so I can feel whole once again.

A Life Changing Day

By Uriel Guerra

The year was 2007. I was in the 7th grade when I joined Carnegie Middle School's soccer team. On the first day of practice the coach told us that he was going to make us run and do some hard exercises. Everything was kind of complicated because I was chubby and the other players were not. The days passed and the coach told me that I had the potential to be a great player, but I just had to practice more and stop eating red meat. The next day I was incredibly nervous because the coach told us that he was going to announce the people that made it to the soccer team.

After school, I was on my way to soccer practice when I saw the coach. I ran up to him and asked him if I had made it to the team but all he said was, "You'll see." When we got to the field he told us to make a small circle in order for him to tell us who had made it to the team. I was really excited and prayed that had made it. So far, all of my friends had made it on the team but the coach still wasn't done with the list. I was in the middle talking to one of the other kids when I heard my name, "Uriel Guerra!" and then "Congratulations! You have made it to the team!" I was so happy to be in the on the team, first of all, because I was going to be with my friends and secondly, because I wasn't going to be sitting on the bench.

The new players played "friendly games" on Saturday's so we could be ready for the tournaments in June. The first friendly game we had was against a team called Barcelona, which we ended up losing, 8-5. The second time we played against Barcelona we beat them by one point, 8-7. The team and the coach were happy because they said that Barcelona was a hard team for anyone to beat. On Monday after school I went to practice and my teammates were still talking excitedly about our win. I was ecstatic because it was my first time playing for a soccer team but what I wasn't happy about was my position. The coach gave me the defender position, but I wanted to be forward because I knew that I could make good passes and score lots of goals. The coach told us that we had to get ready because the day of the tournaments were getting closer, and when the coach told us that we were going to compete against schools with great soccer teams, my heart started pounding harder and harder. Right then, the coach looked at me and asked, "What's wrong with you, Guerra? Why do you have that crazy look on your face?"

I replied, "It's just that I've never played against other schools."

"Don't worry about it," he said. "Just give it your best shot!" The days passed and soon it was the day of the tournament. I was a little scared and nervous because it was my first time playing against another team. First we played Stephen White Middle School and won. Our first victory was 13-5. Stephen White's team was good, but not as good as our team. It was as if our team had already professional soccer players.

Next Monday, the coach told us that we had made it to the semifinals. We were so happy to hear that. The next Saturday came up quickly and we had to go play another school, whose name I've forgotten. By this time, we had lost two games and won three. Finally we came down to our last game. The time was 10:26 and everybody was nervous. The other team scored a goal. Another three minutes passed and they scored another goal. When the first half was over the coach was fired up, and not in a good way. He was really mad! He said "How can you guys let the other team do this to you? You are way better than them. Now get out there and go PLAY. And STOP worrying!" About three minutes after the coach's speech, my friend kicked the ball to one of the players on my team. He intercepted the ball and scored. After he scored the goal the coach praised us by saying, "See, I knew you could do it!" Another three minutes passed and the game was tied.

There were 20 minutes left for the game to end and we already had three goals. My team had the ball and we were just passing it around, until one of my friends, Jose, was passed the ball. While he was running with the ball a kid from the other team trapped him inside the goalie's box and they called it a penalty. The coach told the best player to kick the penalty. Everything was so exciting because there was only two second left, when Jose kicked the ball. When he scored, the other team was really mad. When the goalie kicked the ball the referee said that the game was over, we were jumping around and crying and going crazy because it seemed that we had won the game, 4-2.

We waited for the referee to decide who had won the trophy. We found out that we were going to the penalty phase because we had the same points as two other teams. My heart was pounding hard and my hands were sweating as well. While the coach was choosing who was going to shoot the penalties, we were praying. When he finished deciding, we were just hoping that the people he chose would make the goal. All of the people that the coach chose missed the penalty. The whole team felt as if we were falling into a black hole with no end. Some of us were crying and some of us wanted to but didn't. The coach even said, "Stop crying like little babies!" We did what we could and managed to get 3rd place. The coach was still proud of us because his team had never even gotten 4th or 5th place. We didn't win first place but we all got to play with our friends and have a lot of fun. The next day we had a party in the coach's room where we watched an inspirational movie called "The Dream Begins." Everyone congratulated us and we felt awesome because the boy's soccer team had never even won a first, second, and or even a third place trophy.

Lost and Found

By Karina Garcia

When my cousins and I were about six years old, we were very energetic. The place were we spent the most time at was my house. My grandmother would take care of us while our parents were at work, and we would drive her crazy. I thought she was going to throw fire out her mouth and burn us at any second. We would jump on the soft, yet bouncy beds in my house and sometimes we even broke stuff. Even though my grandmother got angry, we knew she still loved us and most times she was very perky and cheerful. My house was wide. It had more than enough room for us little ones to run around inside. Outside, it was very grassy and lumpy from the spots that we had dug up in the garden.

One day, we were coloring on top of the chocolate colored center table in the living room, when someone decided to play hide-and-seek. My cousin went into the hall closet, which was dark and full of boxes and clothes. In a few minutes, we stopped playing the game because my cousin thought that the box contained our favorite thing ever, --make-up. Every time we would get a hold of make up we would end up looking like clowns, but of course we thought we looked like little princesses. We gingerly grabbed the box, went to the living room, and got ready to discover our treasure.

During this time, my grandmother was cooking lunch for us. I had heard her yell from the kitchen "What are you girls doing?"

We responded quickly, "Coloring!" because we didn't want her to come in the living room and see us playing with make-up. We eagerly got ready to open the old, rusty box and there was no make-up in there. We were all surprised to see a pile of money. We all thought about what we were going to do with money. All of us picked the most reasonable choice of what to do with the thousand dollars we had in our possession, and the most reasonable choice of course, was to buy ice cream!

When my dad came from work, he went straight to the closet and panicked when the money wasn't there. He asked the grownups in the house if they had seen it. Then, he asked my cousins and I and we had to say "Yes" we had taken the money". He asked us where we had placed the money, but we didn't remember. After three hours of looking, my dad found the entire thousand dollars, faded and ripped up in a pile of socks that had just been washed. Consequently, we got in trouble big time. My cousins and I couldn't play with each other for three weeks.

I think this event marked my identity because it made me a different person. It taught me that it always better to return or not touch something you find if it's not yours, and also to respect other people's property. In addition, a person could really need something they have lost. I also learned to not steal my dad's rent money because he will get extremely angry. Lastly, I learned to not be curious about what people have in their hidden boxes because usually, it isn't make-up.

Accelerated Teaching
Career Academy (ATCA)

Lead Teacher: Ms. Rendon
Participating Teacher: Mr. Davidock

MEMORY

By Lara Maria Tiglao

Do you remember?
The day we met
Do you remember?
The pole you stood next to

Do you remember?
The 1st day you spent the night
The way I stole the donuts
And hid them in fake fright

Do you remember?
How we sat and talked
About problems never ending
And laughing without a purpose

Do you remember?
Any of the fights
Do you remember?
How we cried them away

Do you remember?
All those good times
We have had so many
Let's have more

But when I turn to ask you
You aren't sitting next to me
Like always
Guess we've grown up

A Person's Life

By Cynthia Vasquez

A person's life is like a flower beginning to blossom
As kids we are pure,
Like the moonlight and stars at night.
As kids we grow up
With the love of our loved ones.
Like flowers need sunlight and water,
To grow strong and independent
We need happiness and family,
To have the support to be able to grow strong.
Like the flower ready to blossom
We have our freedom.
Like birds can fly in the summer sky
As we become independent
We realize life can be like a lightning bolt
That has consequences for
The decisions we make.
That is the reason we think twice
Before making a decision on
What path to take in life.
Although people get drawn onto the path that looks beautiful,
Because they decide to take the easy way out
Then the time comes when a flower
Loses its color and scent
Like when people begin
To take the last deep breath of air in them.

LOST AND ALONE

By Cynthia Vasquez

Lost and alone
In this big world
There's the north, east, west, and south,
So many directions to take,
But what short lives we live
When lost and alone,
Nobody is by your side
To help you go through the rough times.
Your mind filled up with so many things,
You can't even take a deep breath.
People live their lives about them.
They don't stop to think about
The children out in the world alone
Who suffer every day without food, water and
Sometimes even without their parents.
They feel the cold at night and when it rains
Because of lack of fire or
The holes in their clothes.
But that's not what hurts the most.
It's the love they don't have.
That one video game we really want—
We think we have it bad
When the children out there are suffering
And would do anything to have what we have
Lost and alone.

Basketball Love

By Kelly Tabujara

Our affinity for each other is something that people don't understand.
Let me tell you how it is.

It's like a basketball game, but one that isn't lame.
Where I have to set up the play and make sure everything is okay.

The way he crosses over them other players
Gets me all hyped up in so many different layers.

Let's go back to the summer of 08.
When I would rush in the morning so I wouldn't be late.

He always asked, "Are you comin' Saturday to watch me play?"
And I would be like, "Anything for you and any time of the day."

Every game I went to he would always put on a show.
I would go crazy, but I kept it on the down low.

He would bust his signature move for me, just so I would see.
And he gives me every reason to call him my MVP.

THIS BOY

BY ROCIELLE TABUYO

Wow this boy has caught my attention.
Thinking if he can be more than a friend.
I really do want to get to know him one day,
But would he really think of me the same way?

The things he does make me like him even more.
Especially that one thing that I truly adore.
I just hope that he would try to talk to me,
Even just once, it would make me really happy.

And so that one day came,
Surprisingly he even knew my name.
He said I like you, but I don't know you enough to really like you,
So we decided to get to know each other and see if this can be something new.

We talked as friends as the days went by.
Nothing seemed to happen but why?
At times we would talk but not very long.
It felt like I was doing something wrong.

So at times I would try to move on because we're not a perfect pair,
And it's really hard because even if I try, he's still there.
Trying really hard to move on but he always does something nice,
Something unexpected and it makes me think twice.

He's like different from everyone else out there.
He shows me that he really does care.
Everytime he's near I get really shy.
It's hard to act normal, can you tell me why?

But it's hard to believe that he doesn't even know.
Months have passed and nothing has grown.
I really do like him but then I wonder if I'm wasting my time.
But I know that he's worth it and I will keep trying to make him mine.

HEART BROKEN

BY JODY SAN NICOLAS

I am heart broken.
I wonder if he still loves me.
I hear him whisper I love you.
I see me and him together again.
I want him to love me again.
I am heart broken.

I pretend that we never broke up.
I feel it in my heart that he wants me back.
I touch my heart and it skips a beat.
I worry that some body is gonna take my place.
I cry every day for him to come back.
I am heart broken.

I understand that you can't make a person love you.
I say that if we work out our problems we can make it happen.
I dream of him everyday and hope we will be as one again.
I try my hardest for him to believe me.
I hope he feels the same way as I do.
I am heart broken.

The Wooden Plate

By Jessica Arzola

A sad old man vulnerable to his own age,
He is almost ready to take the next stage.
He is scared and confused,
With no options left to choose.
He cannot speak, he cannot walk,
He's too weak, he's lost it all.

There he sits like any other day,
With his loving family that took him in to stay.
His daughter and her husband and their son of only eight.
He sat with them at the dining table through silence as they all ate.

The old man has a difficult time eating.
He chews loudly and creates a noise that is repeating.
As always he begins to drop his ceramic plates on the floor,
For he was trying to lift the plate but he lost all of his control.
The husband whispers, "I can't take it any more"
As his wife follows him to the open door.
They come back inside and set up a chair
and desk away from the table,
The daughter gets her dad and tells him loudly, "SIT HERE DAD.
IT'S MUCH MORE STABLE!"
The old man sits down in the corner full of shock and disbelief.
He continues to eat and sees that the husband looks more relieved.
He slowly lifts his plate once again to take a bite to eat.
His plate falls and breaks, dropping food all around his feet.

The old man's daughter lifts him up and takes him to his room.
She says good night as she shuts the door
and she goes looking for a broom.
When she gets to the kitchen her husband
starts to complain about her dad.
Little did hey know that the young boy was
still awake listening and starting to get mad.
The daughter went to sleep and her husband stayed up all night.
He was building a plate out of wood
and the young boy couldn't stand the sight.

The old man sat in the corner of the room as he began to wait.
His daughter's husband then served his food
and gave it to him in the wooden plate.
The old man began to eat from it but the food didn't taste the same.
It tasted awful and he knew he shouldn't complain.
His plate then fell down and the young boy picked it up.
The young boy looked at him and he knew
something had to be done.

That night while sleeping the daughter's husband
heard something startling.
He headed downstairs and saw the young boy
with the wood and carving.
He asked, "Son, what are you doing here at this time of night?"
"I was just making something for you and
mom when the time is right."
"Son, you should be going to sleep. It's getting really cold."
"Dad, if I don't build it now, what would
you and mom eat from when you get old?

"You see dad, just like grandpa,
you will have to eat from a wooden plate.
The food may not taste the same, but sorry dad, it's your fate."
The father's eyes begin to swell up and he quickly started to cry.
He couldn't believe he treated grandpa like this,
he couldn't recall why.
He went to bed feeling full of regret and dread.
It was too late though, there was simply nothing to be said.

By Karen Hidalgo

I am friendly and funny
I wonder when the world is going to end
I hear people around me telling me I can't
I see the road to success
I want to achieve big things in life
I am friendly and funny

I pretend I am a pediatrician
I feel hopeful about my future
I touch the stars in the sky
I worry that I won't do much in life
I cry at my grandfather's memory (R.I.P.)
I am friendly and funny

I understand I can't have all I want
I say in god I trust
I dream that the world will have peace
I try to be a better person
I hope I will get to grow old
I am friendly and funny

By Briana Salinas

I am stunned and twitterpated
I wonder if he ever thinks about me
I hear sweet whispers in my head
I see his eyes looking around for me
I am stunned and twitterpated

I pretend I don't care about it
I feel his hand touch mine
I touch the thoughts in his head
I worry that he'll forget me
I cry when he's not around
I am stunned and twitterpated

I understand it's just a dream
I say that at some point it'll never be true
I dream that one day we become one, yet
I try to put it all behind me
I hope he likes me for who I really am
I am stunned and twitterpated

By Cerina Plopino

I am caring and loving
I wonder about life
I hear bells ring
I see the wind
I want to be a successful lady
I am caring and loving

I pretend to smile
I feel your touch
I touch your hand
I worry about school
I cry when I reminisce on the past
I am caring and loving

I understand life is unfair
I say live everyday like it's your last
I dream about a stress-free life
I try to do my best in school
I hope high school is memorable
I am caring and loving

By Diana Morales

I am determined and curious
I wonder what I will be like in the future
I hear people laughing when I walk by
I see life passing by one day at a time
I want to be remembered even after I'm gone
I am determined and curious

I pretend to be a teacher
I feel good when I help people
I touch the stars in the sky
I worry for my parents' health
I cry when I see people suffer
I am determined and curious
I understand that life isn't always fair
I say that there are still mysteries in the world
I dream to be a great history teacher
I try my best to learn new things
I hope to make a difference in the world
I am determined and curious

By Alyssa

I am a nice, brow-eyed girl
I wonder what roams around in space
I hear the ocean's voice calling me to the white, sandy beach
I see my future that lies ahead
I want the life that is full of peace and happiness
I am a nice, brown-eyed girl

I pretend to fly way high in the sky
I feel the sun's rays on my face
I touch the rainbow whenever it comes out
I worry about the cancer that killed her
I cry whenever I remember February 8, 2008
I am a nice bown-eyed girl

I understand how to live, laugh, and grow
I say I am who I am and there's nothing you can do about it
I dream that someday I will see her golden heart once again
I try to get beyond good grades
I hope that people can get along
I am a nice, brown-eyed girl

By Stephanie Galicia

I am generous and talkative
I wonder what is above the clouds
I hear people trying to help me succeed
I see cupcakes flying down from the sky
I want to become a pediatrician

I pretend to take charge of my life
I feel the flowers talking to me in my ear
I touch my future
I worry about when the world is going to end
I cry when I remember something sad in my life
I am generous and talkative

I understand that family comes first
I say always have a positive mental attitude
I dream to succeed in life
I try to do well in school
I hope to get good grades
I am generous and talkative

THE JOURNEYS OF LIFE

By Estefany Orquera

Every life has troubles
The troubles are just temporary
So don't worry
Keep your head up high
Facing the sky
Wipe the tears off your eyes
Forget about the bad past
Smile and say
Everything will be all right
Sooner or later
Your troubles will be gone
And your happiness
Will be the new journey
Of your life

First Love

By Lizabel L.

In sixth grade history class there were fifteen of us in the class. There were only a few girls in the class, five girls to be exact. The rest were all boys. Each and every one of us was shy in the beginning of the semester. It was a small class so we made a strong bond in the beginning. There was this one particular guy named Jim that didn't get along with me. Our classmates tried everything they could to make us closer to each other as friends, but it didn't work. But even though we weren't close, we found ourselves talking to each other.

Around December we had a substitute teacher for our class because our teacher was in a meeting. The substitute teacher had asked me to pass out the worksheet that we were supposed to work on while our teacher was away at the meeting. When I arrived at his seat he blocked me from passing down the aisle. I wondered what had caused him to react like that. After passing out the worksheet I wasn't seated yet, so I took my stuff and sat beside Jim.

"So what was that about?" I asked as I sat down.

"What?!" he replied.

"Um…the way you blocked me?" I replied with a confused look wanting an honest answer.

"Oh that…um, I was asking for a hug," he whispered.

"What?" I asked. He was whispering, and I couldn't hear what he said because the class was noisy as he tried to whisper again.

"You didn't hear what I said?"

"No…Sorry…um, you don't need to say it again if you don't want to," I said. He started writing sentences on my worksheet.

There was a long pause. I turned around and glanced at him. While I looked at him I saw him writing something on a sheet of paper. He looked up, and then our eyes met. It was a long thirty seconds, and then I turned around, blushing for a few seconds.

I continued doing my work after my eyes met his glorious eyes. I was so busy doing my work that I didn't notice there was an origami whale on my desk. I looked up, wondering who put it there. I turned it around and the words encrypted on it said "open it." It lit my face in fascination.

I eagerly followed the directions that were printed on it. I opened it and saw the word "want" within it. After seeing that specific word, it made me more curious. I opened it as fast as I could. Tension within my veins ran through my whole body. My heart was pounding. Then my confused, suspicious face turned into a smile. I started blushing as red as a rose. I turned and saw Jim blushing too.

"Is this from you?" I asked nervously. He looked at me and began to blush and said, "Yes."

After that event, we started talking to each other more and more every single day. We spent more time with each other. Every time we saw each other we gave each other a hug. Many of my friends were surprised at the development in our relationship. No one knew how this had happened. No one even bothered or dared to ask either of us why we were acting as we were.

A few months passed. After that wonderful event I'd realized one thing: I was deeply in love with Jim. He wasn't just another crush; he was my first love. When I realized that inside my heart, I changed. I wanted to be better than I was before. Many of my friends tried to help me out. They worried about me, but I told them that I wasn't going to regret what I've done in the past, ever. I thought I never had to worry about Jim. He was a sweet as honey with chocolate combined.

The second semester came and my whole class changed from a regular class to an honors class. I didn't see Jim that often because I had to do many things, such as homework and projects. I explained my situation to him and he said he understood. Believing this I did my job as a student, but I didn't know that it would also create a change in our lives.

It was like I started first semester again, and we weren't as close as we used to be. We didn't talk very often, and worst of all, inside I knew it was my fault. I grew apart from him. I often thought if we should start hanging out again. But it didn't solve my love problems. I guessed he missed the way we used to hang out, how we hugged and talked. I felt I didn't know him at all as the days passed by.

Later on I realized that he had gotten himself a girlfriend. I felt heart-broken; my world came crashing down. It hurt me like some-one had stabbed me in the back. I was hurt. I should have trusted my friends, but I had ignored them. I had regretted not taking any of my friends' advice. I felt hurt inside, and just like glass being bro-ken, it could not repair itself. Every night I cried in my room, tears of sorrow falling down my cheeks.

I wasn't planning on telling any of my friends. They would ask me questions like "Are you all right?" I didn't want to worry them. I needed some time to face the truth about it, but I told myself that it was OK to love someone even though it was a one-sided love.

After a few weeks passed, I told my friends about it. I felt that it was the right time to do that. They all felt sorry for me, but I had told them not to worry about me or mourn for my lost love.

I learned a lesson, and I wouldn't want to make the same mistake again. We just had different lives, different things to do. Inside, I had found my first love, hoping he was "the one." Knowing I had put school before boys I felt a bit better. I know that I will be the best he never had. Knowing that I will become one of those girls that will become successful in the end. Knowing that I will be better than I was. From that point on I concealed my heart away, and I focused on my studies more than on guys.

Goodbye my first love, I'll never forget you. You're in the mist of my memories, now sealed away in my memories day by day.

Advanced Studies Academy (ASA)

Lead Teacher: Dr. Schuetze-Coburn
Participating Teacher: Ms. Bottlik

Philippines to LA

By Dan Tamayo

I was sitting alone at the middle of an empty room, while staring at the sunset by the window. It was very quiet and calm. All I can hear is the melodic sound of the wind chimes. Thinking that it would be my last time in this room, I closed my eyes and felt the warm breeze coming from the window. I remembered all those good and bad memories I had in this room since I was a kid. All those things I used to have, like those red Ferrari toy cars I used to display by the window are now gone. Tears started falling from eyes, realizing that I'm about to leave a big part of my past. I know that closing a door full of memories is hard, but I need to move on. So I stood up, wiped away my tears, and grabbed the last furniture by the wooden door that says my name. And before I walked away, I said, "These tears in the ground are marks that will last forever."

It's getting dark, so my mom loaded the last luggage bag in our van and asked us to go in. Everyone went in the car except for me. I stood in front of the gate and made a last look at our 2-story white house. It was filled with darkness, and I thought that when people pass by here, they would think of it as a lonely abandoned house. "Dan lets go! We're going to be late and we still have to go to aunt Mimi's house" my sister yelled from my back. So I went inside the car and waved goodbye to my precious house. After about half an hour, we arrived at my aunt's house. My mom parked the car at the back and there I saw my relatives standing at the gate. "Mom, do we really have to move with daddy and sell this house?" I asked.

"He misses us and you miss him too right?" She replied.

"Yes, but..." I said in a low voice without saying another word. Seeing their faces made me run from the car. I talked and hugged each and every one of them for the very last time, and most of them said that they would keep in touch with my family. But the last person I went to and made me cry was the one that I won't forget, which is our maid. She was my best friend and she has been a part of my family since I was a child. It was time to go, but before I walked away, I gave her our family picture and said "Ate, we will miss you".

"Don't worry I'll call you guys as soon as possible." she replied with tears in her eyes. I walked towards the car and sat down at the back with my uncle and waved goodbye.

We finally arrived at the airport. My uncle Bong unloaded all of our luggage and said his farewell to us for the last time and drove away. People scattered everywhere holding big luggage bags. You could hear eerie noises of planes and voices announcing departures and arrivals. I smelled popcorn all over the place because there were food stands all over. All of us were holding luggage except my baby brother. I looked around and I felt a little bit worried because I never been to an airport before. I went through many weird processes, especially this part when inspectors use this scanning machine and check if you have something illegal or harmful. Then we waited at this blue bench where people used to sit until its time for departure. After 2 hours, it was finally time to leave. While walking in the aisle and finding our seats, I told myself that experiencing things you have never done before is kind of fun.

After a long flight, we arrived at LAX. We went through a few processes and grabbed our luggage bags at the carousel. It was very crowded and I noticed how diverse it is compared to our country. It took us a very long time to go out at the arrival area, but when I saw my dad, I thought it was worth it. I hugged him tightly because I hadn't seen him for a long time. He told me that he didn't recognize me at first because I became taller. And as we walked to the parking area, I noticed how cold it is compared to where I came from.

We arrived at my dad's apartment at around 9:00 pm. I jumped my way out of the car with so much excitement. I stood next to my dad's van and for a moment, I noticed all this old cars. And I thought, are we really this poor? But I just ignored it and went to the back of the car and helped carrying our luggage. When I opened the door, I was a little bit frustrated because I wasn't really expecting our house to be this small compared to our house in the Philippines. I checked around the house and noticed that there are only 3 rooms, which means I don't have one. The floor is made of red carpet, there's some old TV's and a computer at my brother's room. Seeing all this things made me realize that we're starting a new life. After unpacking our stuff, and placing it in our rooms, I went to my brother's room and lay down on his bed. I felt a little bit sad because I realized we didn't have a lot of relatives here in L.A. and I was worried that my family would have to struggle. I tried to go to sleep, but I wasn't able to because of the time difference between these two countries and because it was very cold. So the whole night we were awake, and during daytime we were all asleep.

It was the first day of school and my dad dropped me off at Stephen White Middle School. I walked in the gate and saw all these kids in groups waiting for the bell to ring. Some kids stared at me and I felt a little bit awkward so I walked as fast as I could to my class. Standing in front of the door at Room 32, I waited for the bell to ring. My first and second period worked just fine because I only have to share things about myself. But during nutrition, I was worried because I am a shy person and I really don't know where to eat. So I just sat down under this shady tree and ate there alone. While eating, I stared at these people having fun at the bleachers and I felt a little bit frustrated being a loner and I remembered my old friends in the Philippines. Another 2 classes, and the bell have rung for lunch. Well this time, I planned to eat at the bathroom, so that no one would see me eating alone. The bell has rung for sixth period and I felt a little bit sleepy so I rushed to my class, went to my chair and put down my head and waited for the teacher to wake me up. While walking, I noticed that I hard a time concentrating at school because of the time difference. When I came home, I heard my mom and my siblings at the dining room talking about the first day of school. I noticed that we all had the same experiences.

After a year, things started to get better. I was able to meet new friends, which is a very big deal. I was able to conquer my fears and sadness because now we are able to contact my relatives, friends, and our maid in the Philippines. I was able to get and keep my straight A's all the way to 8th grade. And I was able to adjust to all this changes. It was a very tough journey for me and my family. But later on I realized, things will be hard at first, but sooner or later you'll be able to get over it.

Moving On

By Micah Candelaria

I remember a time
When I was first love struck
I was just a child
With a big heart
The moment I saw her
I was hit breathless
With chills down my spine
I just had to move on.

We would always keep in touch
Going to each other's houses
Watching her put on her blouses
Staying up all night
Keeping her in my sight
It was like living a dream
Under a celestial beam
I just had to move on.

Our bond was getting cut short
We had no time for each other
The way it should be
Between two lovers
One heartbreaking day
I see her with another guy
I knew now she was keeping a lie
So I had to do
What most people would do
I just had to move on

REMINISCE

BY KIMBERLY NGOUV

Every time she sees him she looks away
She smiles everyday just to hide from the pain
When she sees them she looks the other way
When she sees him hold her she feels insane
Then she remembers when she was in his arms
The way he'd hold her so close and tight
She can even remember their first kiss
When she sees him kiss her she loses sight
As she looks back she starts to reminisce
Since then she has lost all her confidence

A True Hero

By Neru Hibbler

There my hero stood
As I took my first breath,
I knew that he'd always be here
From birth till death
A short old man,
With a heart of a lion
I still was crying
A true hero

A crazy old man
To have as a grandfather
To others he was mean
To us he was a father
Which was shiny and gold
Bullshit and lies
My grandfather never told
A true hero

There I stood useless
As he took his last breath
A hero, a King, a Chief
A true father till death
But never will I forget
The foundation he's laid
In remembrance of my grandfather
This poem was made
a TRUE HERO

Out

By Edna Ramos

Cocky isn't the way to be
There's more than what meets the eye
That I know deep inside
You're all about ignorance
But what's there to gain
There's a difference and its not being vain
Thinking about being tough
That alone isn't enough
Finding yourself deep within
Is how it'll all begin

The 'It' Girl

By Jazmin Moran-Lopez

Your shy and kind any you make me feel alive
Your like a dream and you seem to breathe life into me
I want you forever in my arms and heart,
You make me feel free like the breeze in spring,
Your voice it toys with my mind, its like music to my ears
My name slips off your lips and it makes me trip
It sounds like a song but my name does not belong
It is dirty and beastly and not worthy to be spoken by your lips
You're so beautiful and brutal, you dazzle at times,
And there are no words to compare to your flair,
You are you; there is no mold no preview
You are free as the wind as I drew you and you flew among
Go be free, fly away, away from the busy streets
And the cloudy skies

INSIDE

By Eduardo Miranda

I though you were the only one who cared about me,
The one who I never was scared to say what I felt,
I thought you loved me, for who I am,
But I guess that you'll never understand

I walk the streets alone, thinking of you killing me inside,
All I wanted to do was be by your side,
And now because of you, I'm scared to love again,
I don't want to be played with and thrown away at the end

I'm trying to express what I feel by words,
But I guess that they'll never be heard,
So I continue to cry, without even knowing why,
I just want to tell you, that I still have something for you inside

I Just Do Not Care

By Kriselle Mendoza

They have a will to kill the joy I have in me
Negatively, they creatively try to persuade me to turn away
It may seem like a bad dream
But no, they just want me red in the head
I don't care about what they won't like
Their problem, not mine
Go ahead and criticize
But my opinion is what will matter in the end, so shut your mouth
And listen to me speak the only answer I seek
I will not listen to the complaints and restraints
you have against my happiness
Because I just do not care

THE PAST

By Karmine Tawagon

A childhood not so bitter not so sweet
A complete family but not together
Friends that may be your friends for show
The rain I saw that day
The meal we had that I can't even taste
The feeling I had of being left behind
The sounds of planes leaving
All these didn't sink into me
Until you left
I cannot feel anything
I am glad there is a weather called rain
Rain that makes me feel nostalgic
Raindrops that remind me of my own tears
You left but I always felt that you're still here
I had friends to spend time and have fun with
I had relatives to make me feel the love of a family
Even if you're far, you're still close in my heart

PAIN

By Celeste Lesure

I wish you could see through my sorrow and through my sadness,
If only you could look beyond the lies and laughter
What would it be like if you looked beyond the smile, I wonder,
Will you ever be able to see beyond the glass,
That veils the vast land of my feelings,
Or will you be blind to the blisters in my body?
Will you feel the fear I face every waking moment,
Or will you turn your back against me and walk away?
You control me at the tips of your fingers,
And your word is my will,
And yet you cannot comprehend what appears in front of you

You

By Nicky Dioquino

My love for you can't be described
But my love for you will always shine
I may not be the perfect guy
But if I can't get your love I'm going to die
At first I didn't like you
But once I saw a glimpse of your smile
I knew deep down in my heart
that I was dying to love you
Whenever I see you smile
I always want to give everything to you
Every night when I close my eyes
I always see your face and smile and realize
Everytime I sleep at night all I do is dream
And make it seem
A picture of us together

LOST BY DISTANCE

BY CELESTE LESURE

I sat on the cold gym floor alone
Eyes wandering for a familiar face
She sat just a ways from me
Looking just as lost as I was
Teachers yelling, cliques gossiping
Sneakers squeaking all around
Initiating the friendship I thought was nailed down:
I confront the lonely girl and thus
We weren't along anymore.
We weren't alone anymore.

In sixth grade, I was overjoyed to be on her team during P.E.
We played football, volleyball, and basketball together
In seventh grade, the girl and I were made partners on kitchen
committee
We sang off key to Feist, and made Cup-of-Noodles
without their pity
Then we attended the Banquet
Garnished in our elegant dresses and jewelry
We ate and danced and danced
And we had the time of our lives
We had the time of our lives.

As I was given the position of Committee chair
I forced a smile to the girl I'd come to care.
She was supposed to become the new boss
But she's moving, I thought at a loss
The day before I chatted eagerly about the position
I told her it would be hers hands down

But her bubbly mood suddenly vanished
And she sullenly told me the news I couldn't accept
I had nearly dropped the cup-of-noodles
And tears formed at the corner of my eyes.
She promised to keep in touch now and then
It's been two years and I still wonder when
Did she break her promise?
Did she break her promise?

Your Last Goodbye

By Katherine Manalastas

Simple daily routines
With familiar faces walking by
Soon interrupted with a new smile
Creating butterflies deep inside
No need for introductions
For I've seen this attractive face in the past before
A very long time acquaintance
Both recognizing the remembrance of ones name
As he whispered a greeting of hello
Which engaged into long conversations
Slowly creating and building a new relationship
Of trust and honesty, and perhaps the silent factor of infatuation
For I've been stabbed by Cupid's arrow
containing the disease of young love
I hope he notices me.

Hugs of comfort and happiness
Walking hand in hand for miles with deep blushes of scarlet
His familiar scent that has now engulfed my senses
Mixed with the ultimate high feeling of a high school crush
Giggles and shouts of debate during the late night phone calls
His intriguing personality that has
grabbed and held my feelings captive
Our trade of gifts holding significant sentimental values
Just the thought of him makes me want to get a heart attack
Our cheesy flirtatious grins that lead
to unforgettable jokes and laughter
As our gazed averted to each other,
wishing the moment can last forever

Comfortable silences are accompanied by his wanted presence
Never pulling away, but staying worthwhile
To enjoy and cherish these moments together
I hope he loves me,

But as the days turned to weeks, and the weeks turned to months
The bold connection that once held us together
Slowly began to lessen and stand on a piece of delicate thread
Awkward silences were now often than usual
Until one particular day, the sun that gleamed in the sky
With it's rays sprawled across my skin, felt not warm at all
His stare was now cold, and he kept
his distance from where I stood
An icy chill rand the back of my very spine
When the hint of sadness and regret glistened in his eyes
And he whispered quiet words that slowly
made my heart shatter and break
The sound of my frantic drumming heartbeat filled my ears
Everything seemed to be a blur as my eyes began to mourn
As he sympathetically turned away without a second glance
For we were no more
I hope he needs me.

THIS IS THE WAY I LIVE

By Shanelle Garrison

I remember when my mom made my sisters and
me sing one of her favorite songs
My mom always told us to stop fighting and get along
I remember when my used to tuck me in at night
I used to stay up and leave on the light
I remember when I didn't like to do chores
But my mom said stop complaining or else you would get more
There were times when I didn't like to go to bed
I used to run around the table like I was out of my head
It felt to me that it was boring
So I got out of the house and got going
I remember when I used to go to the liquor store everyday
I used to laugh and play with my cousin all day
I remember when I used to get spanked
I blamed my sister by saying thanks
I remember when I had my first basketball game
I was upset that I lost, what a shame
Aint no doubt about it is what my uncle likes to say
I enjoy seeing him in church everyday
I remember when I was little I used to say my prayers at night
When I was done I would stare at the stars that were so bright

THE UKULELE THAT SINGS

By Nalani Remigio

The ukulele sings beautiful Hawaiian medleys
As you strum each string,
This little Hawaiian guitar sings,
Lets go, back to your island home across the seas
As you play each song, I know
That all these island songs show;
How to live, with the aloha spirit
In which all these islands give.
And that each song reminds me of,
All the beautiful oceans, people, flowers, and love.
So little ukulele, that sings Hawaiian songs.
Please bring me back to me back to my island home,
where I belong.

Us

By Raken Mai

First find your future create your family
To live with you and to lust with you lovely
Growing old and gaining grey hair; later together in the ground
Please pass these pictures and place them down
Give these gifts to my great grandchildren; their heir
Tell them to take care of it and not let it tear
I want another opportunity to be
able to see you again always amused
Before you go back I want to bring this box it has been abused
It contains a card for the kids to keep; a collaboration
Stay happy don't be sad I'm in your sleep even to this separation

KISS AWAY THE EVIL RAIN

By KATHERINE MANALASTAS

The rain clouds returned and began to reside by the city
Tedious twinkling teardrops of the sky began to pour below
Wet helpless weary citizens withered in the terrible cold
As they asked for the sun to come and
arrive from where it has abandoned
But the bitter bizarre weather blew their hopes away
The rain now poured with more force and power
The stench of wet sidewalks and soggy plants
Filled the faded and frail strangers outdoors
But soon the dark rain droplets grew delicate and dry
The colorless sky's current started to wave clear and calm
The sun's warm rays began to peek through the clouds,
shining and shimmering
Gleaming a glamorous gold and yellow through the solemn skies
Having the people jump and cheer with joy and jolly
For they can now wave the wicked rain clouds goodbye.

The Spark of Love

By Dyllan Thweatt

A small, speculative spark of something special
What a wonderful wish on this world
A bright and bubbling bounding ball of bliss
Conscious crazy collected calming calamity along with
Hindering hiding hysterical happiness
Deep dizzying feelings of fumbling and frustration
Youthful years of yearning
Truly tiring tearful times of turmoil
Merely a magical monstrosity
A true life of love with a twist of loss

My Inspiration

By Ana Hernandez

He's the most important inspiration for all my songs and poems
Though I don't even think he knows this
My heart is amusingly, absolutely attached to the past
Well, it's hard to move on when I cling to what we had
For now I can just write of what I feel when you're far too
And the incredible, indescribable things I felt when I was near you
Remember by that lake how we would
laugh and look into each other's eyes
Inevitably now all I can do is make you
my inspiration because it's all the past
What's the point in thinking of it if we can't change it?
I guess it's remembering the remotely
remarkable things that used to happen
And the way I remember, is by making
you my most significant inspiration

Recalling a Childhood Memory

By Camille Garnett

Oh those beautiful childhood days
How I miss them in many ways

Days in school when I and friends used to run around and play
Falling down and getting back up again every step of the way
Free periods in school when we used to roam around everywhere
Playing tag, hide and seek,and even some games we could not bear

Always eating snacks that we shared very often
Taking naps and playing games in pre kindergarten
With monkeybars and jungle gyms that we would always climb
Intriguing classes where we learned nursery rhymes

Free periods in class where we would play and shout
Always learning new words that we never knew about
Kicking and screaming for our parents not to leave our side
"Mommy, Daddy, please don't leave me" we cried

Rushing out of class to head home from school
Watching teachers teach as they sit on their stool
Finally reaching home, in a total mess
"Why are your clothes dirty," my parents would stress
Now life has begun to increase its pace
Where we are tripping and stumbling to win life's race

Oh, there are times when I wish childhood
days could come back again
For it seems as I've gotten older life has become a real pain

Those beautiful childhood days
How I miss them in many ways

Humanitas

Lead Teacher: Ms. Unzueta
Participating Teachers: Ms. Frank & Mr. Viera

As I Lay Me Down To Sleep

By Sabrina Serrano

I lay in bed with the dried tears on my face
The yelling, the screaming, and fighting
Happening in one place
I was comforted by the sound of your voice
You were the one person
That I thought would never hurt me
The one who laughed, cared, and cried with me,
Turned into another person who I couldn't trust
And ended up hurting me more than I have ever been hurt
Making the hard times I went through, just another day
Who do I go to now?
Even though I see you
I can't make myself look into your eyes
Shoulder to shoulder, we pass each other by
With our happiness no longer in place

By Abby Santandor

As I lay awake in the middle of the night
I start to think about how lucky I am to have you in my life
You've forgiven me for the reckless things I've done
And for me blaming you for all the rough times
You were there for me
Instead of yelling back, you listened
Instead of leaving me in sorrow, you loaned me a shoulder to cry on
You forgave my sinful soul and made me a better person

Change

By Ashley Escobar

I was the one that no father wanted
I remember crying all night asking where he was
I heard that he would never come home
I saw him doing crazy and unhealthy things
I worried that he would die
I thought I would be just like him
But I want to change

I am different from him
I think of what I can become
I need to be more than he was
I try not to think of the past, because it is no more
I feel that he loves me now
I forgive him for all that he did not know
Now I can change

I will try all I can
I choose what will happen next
I dream of doing great in life
I hope I will be all he wants me to be
I predict everything will go well
I know the past will never come back

By Alvin Cabanero

I was a shy, weak boy
I remember losing all my games and toys
I heard many lies
I saw many fights
I worried about people not having rights
I thought my life was going down the drain
But I want to change

I am very smart and athletic
I think the world is too full of violence
I need to stop procrastinating and start to see the light
I try to stop being lackadaisical
I feel heated conversations
I forgive all the hatred and anger
Now I can change

I will be an important part of our world
I choose to be a peacemaker
I dream of a serene society
I hope we will all become better and healthier
I predict change in the world
I know that I can make a difference

By Guadalupe Manzo

I was a girl that had many problems
I remember when people made fun of me
I heard many people say cruel things about me
I saw a lot of discrimination
I worried that my family wouldn't be there for me
I didn't think I was intelligent
But I want to change

I am now a happy and helpful girl
I think everybody has dreams
I need to learn how to speak and write better
I try to do my best in order to show my mom who I've become
I feel happy when my family is proud of me
I forgive my ex
Now I can change

I will be a good, good person in the world
I chose to be a different person by changing my way of life
I dream of being a successful person
I hope that all of my dreams come true
I predict that I will be a good mother and wife
I know I will speak English well soon
I will change....

BY NADIA LOZANO

I was a kid with big dreams
I remember when I lost my friend
I smell a special flower that grows in the mountains
I saw my neighbors laughing
I worried about my neighbors laughing
I worried about how our life was going to be
I thought that I could be perfect
But I want to change

I am a person who thinks a lot
I think everyone struggles
I need to change myself
I try to be a good person
I feel many things that nobody can understand
I forgive somebody that broke my heart
Now I can change

I will change my feelings
I choose to be involved in more activities this year
I dream of being the best friend ever
I hope that this world will change
I predict that I will have a good job
I know that the future may hold problems, but I'll continue to be
strong
I will change

By Claudia Barajas

I was a lonely little girl
Who was raised without a mom or a dad
I heard lots of hateful words around me
I saw people in my family hitting each other
I worried about being alone forever
I thought I would turn out to be a heartless teenager
But I want to change

I am a happy, outgoing girl
I think and understand the world better than I ever did before
I know that I need to study in order to finish my nursing career
I try to make people proud of me
I feel very happy to have my family back
I forgive my mother for leaving me behind
Now I can change

I will become a very successful woman
I choose to follow my dreams
I dream of having my own hospital
I hope that one day, I can get my father to love me as his own
daughter
I predict that I will become a nurse in a prestigious hospital
I know that life is not easy, but I know that I will achieve my dream
of being a good person and living in my own two-story home

By Gabriela Cabrera

I was a girl without any friends
I remember a painful breakup
I heard my sister call me stupid
I saw someone I love get beat up
I worried about my past catching up to me
I thought a certain someone loved me, but they really didn't
I am a girl who is nice and respectful
I sometimes feel like my friends ignore me
I need God to guide me
I try to take criticism positively
I feel close to my family
I forgive my mom for yelling at my dad
I will change in order to improve my life
I choose to look my best at all time
I dream of changing for the better
I hope people won't ignore me
I predict that I will go to college
I know I will graduate soon

By Meiying Ma

I was a young girl from China
I remember not being able to speak a word of English
I heard students fighting
I saw my friends spending time together without me
I worried that people in my family might pass away
I thought that I might turn out bad
But I want to change

I am a nice person
I think that the world can be both good and bad
I want to earn a lot of money
I try to improve my English
I feel joyful because I love learning
I forgive my friends for leaving me alone on my own
Now I can change

I will push myself to attend college
I choose to look nice at school
I dream of becoming rich and successful
I hope to become a doctor
I predict that I will make the world a brighter place
I know that I can inspire many people
I will change

By Judith Ruiz

I was a girl who suffered from depression
I remember my grandmother saying, "I love you."
I heard too much screaming
I saw too much violence
I worried that my parents would see my grades
But I want to change

I am a better person now
I think my friends helped me a lot
I need to finish high school
I try to get help when I run into a problem
I feel like my family has helped me move on
I forgive myself for acting immature
Now I can change

I will finish high school
I choose to go to college
I want to become a teacher in Italy
I hope that I can reach my goals
I predict that I will be somebody
I will change

Unseen Person

By Stephanie Henzon

In my mirror I am an unseen person
I know for a fact that I am there and existing
However I cannot see my face
As if I am in an icy lake
At it's bottomless floor
I reach to catch my reflection on the surface
But all I feel is a glass wall separating us
Try as I might, I cannot reach
For my mind, body, and soul is weak
I know right now that I am in despair
Looking at the face on the other side of the glass I can see
Her face is full of hope and life, nothing that I have
I realized why I can't see my face in the mirror
It's because the person I am now is not the real me

How to Find Narnia

By Stephanie Henzon

Finding Narnia is easier than you think
First, you may have to find the four Kings and Queens of Old
Listen to what they say and do what you are told
Next follow them down a passage that leads to their school
And next thing you know you're in an ocean, nice and cool
Then you help Prince Caspian fight the Telmarines
With the sugar and spices of other Narnians
After the bake, removing the Telmarines out
Keeping Narnia beautiful without a doubt
Finally you leave, for the job is done
You return to where you once started
Even though it's only begun

HOPELESS ROMANTIC

By Maria Fernandez

People think I'm a hopeless romantic
But that's not entirely true
I'm not really that bad
Except when I'm with you

LOVE isn't everything
It's the person you fall for
The one that makes you really feel
Like there's always something more

It's easy to say you love someone
But is she really where your heart lies
To express my love
I would give you all the stars in the skies

I'd give you my whole life
Just to see you smile
Love doesn't make the world go 'round
But it sure makes it worthwhile

Blossoms

By Nicky Reginald Q. Mateo

In my family, I am a weed
A weed in a beautiful field of flowers
I look around and see many colors
The flowers cut me down and tell me I'm nothing
They think I'm gone, but soon...
I grow back taller and stronger than ever
I soon find out that I am a tree
Growing taller and taller everyday
My branches reaching out to the sky
Spring comes after winter
Thousands of white blossoms grow on my branches
I look down at the flowers below me and smile

LIFE AND DEATH

By Brandon Hunt, Ashley Escobar, Dennis Jimenez,
Gregory Vera Cruz, Deric Ramirez,
Alvin Cabanero, and Franz Coronado

Life and death
Night and day
Everything dies
Nothing lives forever
As I watch the hearse drive by
I wonder who died

Life and death
Night and day
As I peeked out the window
There he lay
In the grave, his body left to decay
Life and death
Night and day

I Wish

By Maria Guzman

I wish I could be in a different place
In a different world with a different face
I wish to be at the beach
To see all the fish playing in the sea
I wish I could fly high in the sky
To see the clouds and birds glide so high
I wish I had an apple from a tree
And eat it like a tasty piece of cheese
I wish I could feel free

I was...

By Brandon Hunt

I was an insecure, shelled kid
I remember when my best friend died in front of my face
I heard my mom crying in the other room
I saw a woman being beaten in an alley
I worried about if she would need medical attention
I thought I would end up just like my uncle
But I want to change

I am outgoing and intelligent
I think we live in a cruel world
I need to buy my mom a house (just like I promised her.)
I try to settle down
I feel like throwing away the smile on my face
I forgive you, bro. Rest in Paradise "J.B."
Now I can change

I will be an educated college graduate
I choose to dress as if I were born in the 80s
I dream about the lady in the alley all the time
I hope to become the greatest ballplayer I can be
I predict getting a sports scholarship to college
I know that I will be a successful husband, father, and son

TIRED OF BEING STRONG

BY ANONYMOUS

When they fight my heart starts aching
It hurts so bad, I start shaking
Living with all this tension and stress
Some say, "No wonder she's depressed."
Living in hell may not seem so bad
So maybe you can teach me not to be sad
I just want to live a normal life
With someone to guide me from wrong and right
I'm tired of being strong for everyone else
While struggling to find my true self
Leaving the past behind and trying to move on
Why does everything seem to turn out wrong?
Hiding my face behind my hair
Won't help me avoid all the mean-ass glares
Stab my heart and open my mind
Hide the key and turn back time
I'm sick and tired of all the blame
I look in the mirror and feel ashamed
I look under the rainbow and find the gold
I take that risk and become bold
I rub the shiny lamp and get three wishes
Sparkly like my vintage dishes
I want to be noticed, accepted, and loved
Given attention—maybe a kiss, or a hug
I'm tired of simply wanting all these things
Can't I just start over without any sins?

Sister

By Ysrael Hernandez

You put ketchup on my clothes
So I put mustard in your shoes
Even though you messed with me from time to time
I still feel that I turned out fine
We matured and got older
We continued to get bolder
We still yell, we still fight
But you bought me new shirt
So now it's all right

∞

Forgiveness

By Gabriela Aceves

Should I forgive you
After all you did to me
Should I forgive you for telling me lies?
Should I forgive you for making me go through so much pain?
Should I forgive you for making me cry thousands of times?
Should I forgive you for all those times you said you loved me
But never meant it?
Should I forgive you for not being there when I needed you?
I went through so much in my life because of you
And for that, I will never forgive you

PERSPECTIVE

By Courtney Wells

As I fly I see
What comes for me
Raindrops, heat waves, and prey for those to eat

This job of flying is daunting
And haunting too
I mean, what would you do?
If all these elements were after you?

It takes time to adjust
Although I must say
It wasn't easy to stay
Being that I'm prey
For the everyday
To live and for those to eat
Life must be sweet
For those who come after me

LIFE STORIES

BY COURTNEY WELLS

Life is a story that should be told
As you go through it, many stories unfold
When you get through the hardships, your storms may cease
Yet they continue to arise, just like a beast

As time passes, life gets easier to bear
Since you stop giving a care that everyone is in your hair
They come around like no tomorrow
Because they haven't learned to overcome sorrows

Life stories are like an open book
Every story has a hook
As seasons come and go
They begin to rhyme like so

Life stories are like English—
Written words containing verbs
Which are used to express
All of my life stories best

Imperfect

By Abby Santander

Some look but do not see
Tree branches sway gracefully with the wind
Birds fly oh so high, almost parallel to the clear blue sky
Kids running carelessly
Laughing, sounding oh so jolly
This world seems to be a demonstration of absolute perfection
But if one searches, they will see, this would be
What one may call imperfect
Scattered cigarettes, affecting the lungs of little ones
Cars, polluting the air we breathe
Heartless people, taking advantage of the innocent
This world is imperfect, but we are too blind to see
That perfect is what you and I can never be

ROLLERCOASTER RIDE

By Abby Santander

In reality, this life is a rollercoaster
In the beginning it has its excitement, thrills, and mystery
Throughout the ride, it gets bumpier and bumpier
And it has its ups and downs that are full of joy and misery
At the end of the ride, the excitement goes away
It becomes calm and just right
Life is a rollercoaster
No one knows what life has to give you until you hit the end

WRATH

By Abby Santander

The wrath within dissolves
As I   hear
That soothing sound   The sinful stress fade
S Never to come around   The rhythm runs
Through my brain   like adrenaline rush
Ing through my veins   it's me   the mirror and
The dance floor   I feel a   righteous isolation
The only chemistry   between   the music and I
Only true passion could   only apprehend...

ROAD SIGNS

By Bryanna Gutierrez

Every summer was the same
We'd take a road trip to a new place
Habia cinco personas en el carro de mi mama
Still tired from rising early
The drive was often silent
Since everyone was tired and weak
Yo tambien tenia sueno y mis pensamientos se piensa a volar
But I kept myself engaged in the road signs
Each sign was similar but not quite the same
They were still so different but all had an important message to
convey
They were not the most intricate objects in the world
But they sure caught my eye
And to tell you the truth
Es un memoria que me quedo

Loving Dreams

By Bryanna Gutierrez

In my dreams, I am music
My sweet melody shows you the way home
The music notes I read
Are the signs that bring you closer to me
The rhythm of my song sets you free
My lyrics share with you the stories I have to tell
When you are finally home with me
I know that all is well
Because our hearts beat to the same tune
And our song sounds like this....
"I love you"

How to Get a Girl

By Desiree Pineda

How to get a girl…
There are many way to start…
#1: be careful, don't be like the other guys and break her heart
#2: don't give her little pickup lines that you find on Myspace
#3: spitting game through AIM won't be easy as tying a shoelace

See now, girls remember everything you say
And trust me, your friends already know about her at the end of
the day
Girls like it when you're straight up and real
So don't come at her talkin' this and that about your little "sex ap-
peal"

Don't take her for granted and think she's easy to get
'Cause a wise girl will leave before she's LEFT

Battery

By Arra Ramualdo

In my fears I am a battery
I don't know how much I have left in me
I have used up most of my energy
I want to be long lasting
I just want to be happy
And march to the beat of my own drum
Right alongside the Energizer Bunny

Untitled (A found language poem)

By Arra Ramualdo

Women seek true non-stop love
Passing back hopes
Fighting out energy
Warnings ignored
Counting faces down life
Crossing new timing

Curtain Call

By Antonette Penalba

I came to watch a play about memories
Because in the past I was a happier girl
A girl without a care in the world
I smiled more, laughed till I cried
But now instead, I just frown and sigh
Pokemon marathons and campfires
Some of the memories I admire
But today, it's not the same
All disappointment and shame
People who came, now have to go
So I guess it's time for the end of the show
But I wish for another callback
So I can re-live those times and get back on track

∞

I am the sun

By Jerwin Balon

Lighting up her life
I am the eagle, hovering around to protect
I am blue, with peace over new
I am glue, putting things back together for you
I am happy, for my life is with you

Leadership Academy

Lead Teacher: Mr. Stevens
Participating Teachers: Ms. Kasuyama & Mr. Santelman

By Gabriela Garcia

The wind blows everywhere
In the trees, in your hair
I see the month of May.

I walk across the grass
And find myself lost
In the hot, hot heat

Falling to the ground,
I see a leaf fall down,
In a pile of brown.

It's freezing—so I wait
For something to help me
And take me somewhere.

I hear cracking and crunching
Of today's fun day
And it won't last

So I leave it alone
And hope for the best
This new day.

ACROSTIC

By Nicholas Flores

Flowers blooming, kids are playing.
Land is greener, let it rain
Over the mountains, and in the skies
Rivers flowing, looking through my eyes
Evening's now, dark is near
Summers coming, it will be clear

∞

FEAR ME DEAR, FOR DEATH IS NEAR

By Stephanie Monroy

Feeling your kisses,
Loving the way you love me,
Our time is now done.
Kiss me one last time for death
Is near and coming for me.

By Mariza Calarana

You tell me we can
Do whatever we want
Now you say we can't
It's not possible for me
To leave you here almost dead.

∞

LIFE'S WHAT YOU MAKE IT

By Lusia Togia

Living life like there's only today
Understanding how I can make it fun
So I turn to my friends without dismay
In boredom we drain, each creating a pun
As we laugh with each other saying, "You just made my day."

DEADLY LOVE

By Heidy Pinto

He is the power of my love
Ecstasy to my body and soul
If he weren't here…there is
Deadly rush in my veins
You are the border between life and death

Pity for the damned
Inside the living hell
Negative thoughts of death through our minds
Taste of evil and…
Opposing to love.

THE FLOWERS

By Shyann Hale

The flower's beauty
Is like the sun at setting
It shines so bright

My Little Poem

By Otilia Marquez

Everything seems to be jumping out at me,
& so much that I can't see.
I just want to bury all of my thoughts,
& not have to worry
things get better
& some things get worse
like the times you want to burst
when you want to get down and cry
& just when you're about to say goodbye
You say to yourself
"Someone out there wants to be alone and
you're the only one that keeps them sane."

Spring

By Edgar Picazo

After a cold month
Seeds become flowers and they
Are ready to bloom

.

Haiku

By Josephine S.

The girl laughed freely
As she talked with her cousins
Oh, how she loves them.

❀

Haiku

By Keaton Stewart

After a hot month
Seeds tend to force up
And are ready to pop.

❀

Tanka

By Joshua Gabriel Isip

I walk straight along
With fear stepping on my back
I'll try to be brave
But my sight seems to be gray
And still I'll try to be brave.

Haiku

By Jethro Rivera

Happy like the sun
Sweet like the bird's swinging voice
Oh, it is spring time.

Soccer

By Ruben Real

Soccer is a game of men and women
Girls and boys all over the world
Race don't matter but your game.

POEM

By Fabian Renteria

There once was a man named Frank
He owned a national bank.
But soon he realized he would repent
Because the economy put him without a cent
So from there everything went down
And now he begs for money with a frown.

HAIKU

By Cherrie Hermano

Always part of life
Tells you who you really are
Best friends forever!!

FLOWER

By Kimberly Naval

Touching the green grass
Drips its dew to the ground
Like a tear it falls.

132

My Poem

By Kimberly Martinez

Roses are red
Violets are blue
I'm so glad I found you.
The sky looks as blue as the ocean.
I hear the wind blowing
But I can't hear.
I can't wait to have you in my arms
And tell you I love you.

By Maria Hernandez

George sees a dog
But remembers never talk to strangers
The dog jumps on a log
Meanwhile George sees a jungle ranger.

By Marlen Hernandez

The monkey climbs high
The monkey climbs low
Trying to catch that pie
Oh my—he just hit his toe.

∞

Tanka

By Stephanie Carranza

Beautiful mountains
Rivers with cold, cold water
While cold snow on rocks
Trees over the place with frost
White sparkly snow everywhere.

Tanka

By Pamela Camacho

The cat in the hat
Is very funny to read
Little kids always enjoy
As for me I always have fun
But I am not a little kid.

LITTLE BROTHER

By Christopher Carrillo

An event that has impacted my life is the birth of my four and a half month old brother. He was born on December 1st of 2004 at 5:17 pm. It was a Monday. Usually Monday's are a real drag for me, but this was soon to be the best Monday of my life! I was so excited and tense to meet my new little brother for the first time. I had waited for this moment for many years. At certain points of time during that day, I didn't want to go to the hospital to meet him because I was so scared and nervous that something bad was going to happen. But thankfully everything turned out well.

So I toughed it out and went to the hospital to visit my new baby brother. When I got to the hospital I was scared to take the elevator up to see him. I had butterflies all in my stomach, and I never felt this way before. I was very excited! This was an important moment for me; this changed my life in many ways. For example, he made me want to be more helpful and useful around the house since he was so tender and small. This little boy will look up to me for all the answers a big brother can give from this day forth. It is an incredible responsibility but I think that I can be the best big brother and role model for him.

I have to be the man of the house and live up to my responsibilities as his role model now. I need to get work done in school. Also, must behave at home and help my mom out around the house. Even though I am not the only child now, this impacted me in positive and fun ways. I can teach him how to play sports, and teach him about other things that I know. This excites me because I get to share my knowledge and what I know about life with him, and teach him the things that he is going to need to know later in life.

The birth of my new baby brother has had a major impact on my life, school, and especially at home making choose smarter and better options in life as life puts forth everyday. This was a very exciting and impactful moment for my family, but especially for me.

Letter From a Friend

By Nadia Mageo-Li

I just had to write to tell you how much I love you and care for you. Yesterday, I saw you walking and laughing with your friends; I hoped that soon you'd want me to walk along with you too. So I painted you sunset to close your day and whispered cool breeze to refresh you. I waited—you never called—I just kept on loving you.

As I watched you fall asleep last night, I wanted so much to touch you. I spilled moonlight onto your face—trickling down your cheeks as so many tears have. You didn't even think of me; I want so much to comfort you.

The next day I exploded a brilliant sunrise into glorious morning for you. But you woke up late and rushed off to school—you didn't even notice. My sky became cloudy and my tears were the rain.

I love you. Oh, if you'd only listen, I really love you. I try to say it in the quiet of the green meadow and in the blue sky. The wind whispers my love throughout the treetops and spills it into the vibrant colors of all the flowers. I shout it to you in the thunder of the great waterfalls and compose love songs for birds to sing for you. I warm you with the clothing of my sunshine and perfume the air with nature's sweet scent. My love for you is deeper than any ocean and greater than any need in your heart. If you'd only realize how I care.

My mother sends her love. I want you to meet her—she cares too. Mothers are just that way. So please call on me soon. For if you want me to, I'll make you whole. But I'll only do it if you say so. I'll never force you, for I love you so. I'll give you freedom—is it yes or no? No matter how long it takes I'll wait—because I love you.

I'm Sorry I Can't Tell You What

By Nadia Li

I'm sorry I can't tell you what
I'm sure you'd rather hear,
Cause there's a burden in my heart
I can no longer bear.

Before I come to you
And make my peace with you
There's an anger I must cross

I know I wasn't what you wanted
When you wanted me.
And you never understood what I am
But I would not be me without you.

You were sorry, first for me
And then for you, and wept,
And turned from its embrace.

Ah, how you injured me
By what I would become,
To love myself I had to leave
And make my way alone.

I needed but a different road
To reach the common goal
And rather than accept that life
Of what I would become.
But always, always looking back
To where I had no home.

Goodbye Mom

By Cristeena Iakopo

I was in the sixth grade and so was my cousin Logan, and I was thirteen years old. We were all at school taking a test, and my uncle came and had to take us to the hospital.

At first, I was wondering what was going on; I wanted badly to ask, but I didn't because I knew I was going to cry so I kept my mouth shut and didn't say anything at all. When we arrived at the hospital, I just wanted to go straight into my mom's room and stay with her all day and never want to leave her side. After, when my auntie said it was okay to go up there, I just went straight up to her room with my brother Joshua. When I got up there, I just grabbed a chair and sat beside my mom's bed and just held her hand and told her that I loved her so much and she was the best mom in the whole world.

More of my aunties and uncles started to show up and came inside the room. Most of us were in the room while some were just standing in the hallways or outside smoking. It was getting late, it was around five o'clock and some of us were getting hungry, so my auntie and uncle took the kids to Hometown Buffet across the street. I didn't really feel like eating at that moment, so I decided to stay at the hospital because I was too depressed to eat. They came back around six o'clock and we all just sat inside and outside of the room.

I knew that the moment was coming and I could feel it rush through my head to my toes. I felt like I couldn't breathe; I wanted to cry so badly, but I just held it in, so I asked my Auntie Teri to come outside with me so I could get some air. While we were outside I asked her, "Why did this happen to my mom? What did she do wrong to deserve this?" I just looked up into the sky and prayed to

God, saying, "Please make her healthy. Look at all the sad faces!" I just turned to my auntie and started to cry.

After that I calmed down, and my little cousin Myah was singing to my mom. While she was singing she was crying so she made me cry again. My other cousin, Nunu, just looked at me and told me to stop crying, and I couldn't because how could I stop crying when somebody I loved so much was in the hospital dying?

The moment came. God sent an angel down telling my mom it was almost time. Everyone had said their goodbyes and gave their hugs and kisses. When my dad came, we looked at each other and I put my head down. He held my mom's hands for about thirty seconds, and left the room. I looked at my mom and dropped down in tears. I couldn't stop crying. My whole life seemed to just drop, and my heart ripped into little pieces. I just hate the thought of looking at one of my family members lying dead in a casket; when I think of it, I just start to cry.

I woke up the next morning just hoping this was all a dream, but it wasn't. I got up and took her picture off my mirror and just looked at it and started to cry, and placed the picture beside me as I went back to sleep. I woke up around ten because we all stayed home. We really didn't feel like doing anything.

The next day I really didn't feel like talking to anyone at school, so I just sat by myself and just said to myself that my mom was in a better place and she will be proud of me and my brother. My mom's death changed my whole life. It has been almost three years that my mom has been dead and I still can't get over here death. To me it seems that I didn't complete something, something that will help me get over it. If I ever find that something, I will try to complete my feelings, let them leave my mind, and just live strong.

Everyday, I just think about her and just want to spend one last time with her and make it last forever. I would tell my mom how much I love her, and thank her for bringing me to this world, and also that there is no one in the world who could ever take her place. My mom was like my best friend and there is no one that could ever be like the greatest mom in the world, and that person is my mom. My mom was a very caring person. She loved kids so much and she always would have time to spend with her nieces and nephews no matter what she had to during her own time.

My life changed so much after my mom's death. I just really can't explain it, but it just seemed to affect my life and it's holding me back from doing what I want to accomplish in life.

Moira Ann Iakopo
May 13, 1966 – May 2, 2006
Rest in peace Mom

DIVORCE

BY BRENDA PLASCENCIA

My name is Brenda Plascencia and I am fifteen years old now. When I was eleven years old, my parents separated. It had a very big impact on my life. At first, I lived with my dad. He took care of me really well even though I wanted to be with my mom but I felt that my dad needed me more. The whole thing with my parents at first didn't really affect me because I was still pretty young and I didn't really know what was going on.

A year after that, my dad decided that his girlfriend was going to move into the house. Everything just happened so fast, but yet I was happy because my dad wasn't going to be alone anymore. The lady seemed nice at first. She had two daughters; one was fifteen and the other was sixteen. They were older than me and I was happy because I was going to have to big sisters to learn stuff from. Everything was going great at first: my dad was happy, my older brother seemed happy, and I guess I was happy myself. But inside, I wasn't. I wanted my mom, not that lady, to be there trying to take my mom's place in the house.

As time passed I started to dislike that lady more and more. She tried to act like she was my mom. I never told my dad how I felt because I didn't want to cause him any problems. Her daughters started to act bossy and were always trying to tell me what to do. Soon I became tired of all that nonsense and couldn't take it anymore, but yet I still didn't say anything to anyone except for my best friend, Patty. I would cry and let everything out with her. She was still like my sister. She still is. She would always be there for me when I needed her.

During that time, my parents went to court to divorce. The judge asked them if they were sure of what they were doing and if there was any possibility that things might be able to work out between them. They didn't divorce; they talked things through, and decided to give it a shot to be together again.

Things were going good, but then everything started to change again. Things were going wrong again. Before I knew it, they were separating again. This time, I left with my mom. I didn't know why, but I didn't feel the same way as living with my dad. Maybe it was that I was used to being with him. But now, everything is good because they are finally back together.

THE BEST BIRTHDAY EVER

BY BRANDY BURKHEAD

It was July 20, 2004, and it was my ninth birthday. That day it was like any regular day. I woke up, ate breakfast, and went to school. My mom wished me a happy birthday, and dropped me off at school. I was at school and I was very anxious. I told my friends that I thought there was going to be a big surprise for me when I got home.

At lunch, my friends and I were trying to figure out what the surprise was. We couldn't figure it out. We were thinking that my mom got me a puppy. I thought she got me a bike. Then in class, they told me I had to leave early.

I went to the office and left with my mom. She had balloons and a huge cake for me. When I got home, my mom sent me to our neighbor's house. At three o'clock, she came and got me. When I went in the house, everybody was there. I was so happy!

I got stuff that I never expected to get. I got a flat-screen T.V., an iPod, a gold necklace, gift cards, a bike, and $165. That was the best birthday ever. I will never forget all of the things I got.

DEATHS IN THE FAMILY

BY KENDRA CURRIE

A time that had impacted my life was when I had lost my grandma and niece. It had influenced a big part of my life, because when I had lost them, everything started to change. Things like family get-togethers weren't the same without them.. I remember when I used to go visit and help my grandma out every Saturday.

Without them, my life is not the same. There are times when I have flashbacks and there are times when I think about the good things we used to do and share. There was a time when I didn't have anyone to go to when I needed help, but my grandmother was always there for me. I would never forget the last words she spoke to me before she passed away. This is what she said, "I want you to finish up school and be something in life."

Ever since then, I strive to do the best I can in school, because if she were here, I know, that would make her happy. Although she is gone, I will never forget about her. She passed away before her eightieth birthday. She loved a pretty good long and healthy life. I hope that I am able to live to that age or past that age. I think that it would be good to have a good life and live a long life.

My niece didn't get to make it past twenty-five. She was killed when a bullet had come flying through her head and taken her life. If she was still here, I know that she would be glad to see her daughter again and finish medical school.

Now that they are gone, I know that they won't have to worry about people getting killed, car accidents, and other tragic things that could happen if they were still here. I would say that now it's time for me to start being thankful for every moment I breathe, because I never know when it will be my time to go. I would also like to say that there were more deaths in my family, but those are the main two that made a big difference in my life.

My Thirteenth Birthday

By Cory Negley

Well it all started the day of my thirteenth birthday, July 12, 2007. That day was so fun and incredible. Mostly all my friends were at Perry Park. It is a small park near my house that not a lot of people know about. My girlfriend came also, because she lives near me. We had a lot of pizza, and a lot of sodas, too! We all ran around and did kid stuff. Then we all gathered around and played football, but the girls did not want to play. My team won, but it wasn't that easy because the score was thirty-six to thirty-three. The game lasted about an hour.

Everything was going perfect. After the football game, we ate pizza, but then my friend, Chris, started to "pizza-slap" everyone! It was funny, but that wasn't how I planned it. It made everyone laugh, so I was okay with it. Then, out of nowhere, we started a soda war! It was a waste of soda, but everyone was involved in it. My girlfriend got the most soda on her. She was all sticky and her hair was tangled. I felt bad. She said it was okay, "It was fun, though." Then my friend Chris and I pulled a prank on my girlfriend with the ice chest that the sodas were in. The sodas were gone, but the water was still in there. So we picked it up when she wasn't looking and spilled it on her. It was a hot day, so she really didn't care. I wrote about this because it didn't turn out the way I wanted, but it was still very fun.

CHRISTMAS

By Gabriela Avila

My favorite holiday is Christmas. It is important for us to celebrate it because it was when Jesus was born. For Christmas, the whole family gets together and we all bring some delicious food. At twelve o'clock we all start to open our presents. I just like it when we all get together. We've been doing this every year. It's really cool because we put on music and we dance, then we take a lot of pictures, and talk. The little kids play there games. Every Christmas that passes by, all I do is watch T.V., play, dance, and talk with my cousins. During Christmas, I see the whole family: all my uncles, aunties, cousins, and even my grandma. I like the decorations that we put up. I also like the lights from the outside of the house.

The thing that I don't like is that during Christmas time it is either raining of freezing outside. But when it is, we warm ourselves up by turning on the heater or drinking something warm. By the end of Christmas, I thank God for everything: For letting me be with my family, and for giving us what we have. I just hope that I get to see the same thing every year when I get older. I am always happy when it comes to Christmas. Even about my uncles when they start drinking.

What we usually make are tamales, horchata, cakes, and many other good foods. My favorite part is when we go shopping for presents. I always end up getting a gift card or money. I always buy my family a present. Well, we give each other presents.

I just hope to see the same thing every year.

THINGS I LIKE

BY RICARDO VERA

Hello, my name is Ricardo Vera. My authentic birth date was in the year 1994 on June 23. In my family there are a total of four children. In order, I am the second oldest child in the family. The oldest child is Miguel, Jr. and his birthday is October 23, 1986, then me, Andy whose birthday is April 3, 1999, then Evelyn born on November 6, 2000. My father is Miguel Vera and my mother is Ana Vera. I have twenty cousins and twenty each of uncles and aunties.

I remember that I went to Hawaii with my godfather and godmother. When we got there we looked all around the island of Maui. The beach was nice because the water was clear blue. Then I went in the water. The water was warm and very nice. Then I went on the jet skis. It was cool because we were going very fast on the waves. Then the next day we went to see how the Hawaiian people cook the pig under the ground. We got to eat some of it and it was so delicious.

I value my friends because they are there for me when I need them to help me with my homework. My friend Luis tells his father to take me to school everyday and he makes sure that I am in school on time and do my class work. Then my friend Danny is always there for me when I need him. Danny helps me with my computer when I need to know some things I don't know. He taught me many things about the ink and hard drive.

At my mom's job they always get a special events for the entire family. They always get some tickets for Six Flags, Disneyland, soccer games, and Knott's Berry Farm to have fun. We always ask for twenty tickets so we can give them to my aunties and uncles.

I like to go to work with my big brother and my dad, so I can make some money so I could buy a nice big house. I like to play soccer and baseball. I like to go out of town like Mexico, Hawaii, Puerto Rico, Texas, and Washington D.C. I like to travel everywhere so I can meet different people.

Important things I have learned are to get good grades and education to stay in school. I need to finish high school and college so that after I can find a good job and make good money. I learned that my family is important and valuable so that I can be happy.

My Two Sisterns

By Ruben Placencia

The thing that has impacted my life is my two little sisters, America and Kayla. Before, when I was an only child, I could watch any program I wanted and now I have to watch Barney with my sisters. What I enjoyed the most before my two sisters came was to be in my room with no one making noise and interrupting my programs. I could concentrate on doing my homework without any babies interrupting me.

Every time I got something to eat I would eat it all by myself. Now I have to share because if I don't my two sisters will start crying and it is very annoying because they will get me in trouble. I also was able to take a nap without getting slapped in the middle of my sleep by my sisters. I used to go to the theater and watch the movie of my choice. Now I either watch a little kid movie or get interrupted by my sisters while I am in the theater.

I used to drive in the car with my mom and hear my music, but now I have to listen to Strawberry Shortcake songs. I also like staying in my room by myself with my door closed but my mom tells me not to close it because she wants to see me spending time with my sisters.

The thing that really upsets me is that before my sisters were born my mom used to buy me things. Now she buys Pampers. My mom doesn't have enough money to buy me things that I want.

My mom asks me to watch the girls while she is doing chores and that really gets on my nerves. I also have to wash their bottles and entertain them while Mom is cooking. I don't think it is fair that I have to start earning my own money to buy myself things and also to pay for my own cell phone.

When My Grandma Died

By Hodari Wells

A personal event that has impacted me is when my grandma died. I was only seven years old and I didn't understand what had happened. My whole family was in the house because she had cancer, and everybody was crying. The paramedics came and they came out of her room with a black bag. I saw my mom cry for the first time, and I saw my mom trying to stop the paramedics from taking that black bag. Now I know it was my grandma they were taking.

I was so confused because I didn't know what was happening or I didn't understand what was happening, but yet I thought to myself, "Who is going to take care of us?", because my grandma was our caretaker. After that day everything changed. I was left with my aunt and uncle; just me and my brothers and sisters. As we got older, we started to understand life more and more because life became so different. When I was with my grandma, the whole family came over to the house to party and have fun, but after she died, my family started to come over less and less.

Now all of my sisters have moved out, and now it's just me and my brother. They treat him like he is a little kid or something, but he's not; he is twenty-one years old and goes to college to learn to be a welder. Sometimes I think that it's good that I stay with my aunt and uncle because they have discipline. If I had stayed with my grandma I would have been in a gang or jail or dead. I was seven years old and would stay outside until the next day.

So, really, I am happy I got placed in their custody because they taught me that life's not fair until you make it. To that I say, "Thank you", because it has really impacted my life and the way I look at people sometimes.

Off to Florida!

By Maurice Johnson

On summer vacation in June 2002 was the year my family was going to Florida on a vacation and I was greatly excited to be going on a plane for the first time. I was eight years old and my dad wanted to take us to Florida to go to Disneyworld because he told me and my brothers that they have the largest Disneyland in the world and they have four parts to the theme park.

My family got packed to leave three days early so we wouldn't rush to get out of the house and make our plane on time. We were going to Florida for seven days. The day before we left California was a big day. My dad had a lot of errands to make sure everything was taken care of before we left. My mom was cleaning the house because she hates leaving the house dirty whenever we go somewhere for a long period of time. My two brothers and I were much excited because it was the first time we would be on a plane. At about six o'clock at night, we had to go to bed so we could be rested enough to be ready in the morning.

At approximately five o'clock the next morning, we all woke up to get ready because our plane was leaving at nine-thirty am. So we all jumped in the shower and got dressed to leave. My mom made us some cereal and we ate it while my dad was putting our luggage in the truck so we could eat and be on our way. Me and my brothers finished eating and went to the car while my parents did a check to see if we had everything. While I was in the car, I told my brother that I was excited to finally be going on a plane. I was a little bit scared that I would get plane-sick or the plane would crash. I had seen too many movies where a plane crashes and everyone dies from an elevated fall.

My parents got in the car and my dad started driving. I asked my dad if he knew how long we were going to be on the plane and he said about six hours. I was flabbergasted at his answer because it's hard for me to sit that long because I am very fidgety. He then told me that there were many things the flight attendant can give your to do on a plane.

We got off the freeway and went to LAX airport and at about eight forty-five am we parked the care, got our luggage, and walked into the airport. My dad picked up the tickets and the lady told us to go to Gate 33. At about nine am we saw a line at the gate where a lady was taking tickets. We all went to the line and my dad gave the lady five tickets. The attendant told us to put our bags in this tiny mechanical door that slides, and to walk through a checkpoint to get searched for weapons before going through the gate.

So we went in a long hallway leading to the plane door. As I was walking in the hallways, I was so excited and anxious that I felt like flying the plane myself, but of course, I was only eight years old. At the end of the hallway, we went in a door, looked around, and saw that we had made it. There were lots of seats and I saw passengers putting bags in a cubby hole above the seats. We found our seats and my mom and dad put their bags in our cubby. The flight attendant told us through a microphone that the plane was about to take off, so to put on our seat belts and enjoy the ride to Florida. I put on my belt and my mom strapped in my baby brother, and made sure me and my big brother were settled.

I saw a TV above me but it didn't have sound. My mom said I would have to plug in earphones to listen. On the armrest I saw about five buttons; volume, channels, and a green one the said attendant. The plane took off and we were very high in the sky. I was kind of frightened because we had some turbulence, but I got a hold of myself. I took out my bag that I had my coloring books, Gameboy, books, and puzzles my grandma packed for me.

A couple of hours later I saw a flight attendant gong around with a cart with food and drinks on it, asking people if they were hungry. By the time they got to us my parents got some spaghetti. My little brother was asleep, so my big brother and I got spaghetti, too, and apple juice. As we passed other states going into Florida, I fell asleep with the earphones in my ears. When I woke up, there was a blanket over me that the flight attendant had given me when I was asleep.

I became bored, so I began coloring while my brother did my jigsaw puzzle. After that, I was on my Gameboy for about an hour and my eyes were so tired from looking at the screen for so long, I turned it off and rested for a while. Then the flight attendant said we were going to land in Florida and to gather our belongings. Once we landed, we unbuckled our seat belts, and twenty minutes later we got off the plane. In the lobby, my dad asked my brothers, "How was your first plane ride?" I told him it was cool, and I couldn't wait to have another one!

Performing Arts and Media Academy (PAMA)

Lead Teacher: Mr. Greenwood
Participating Teachers: Mr. Cox & Mr. Greenwood

When I Think of You

By Justine Penesa

Every time I think of you my heart fills with joy,
like the feeling I get when I am with a boy.
Everything you've done for me I'll never forget,
like the time I was little and how you put me to bed.
I remember the times we used to share,
 and how you always told me how much you cared.
I think of the times when I was young,
 how we used to go places and have so much fun.
When I was little we used to play
 reliving those days I never thought I'd say,
 that I'm missing you so much as I live each day.
 Just the thought of you gone. I'm wishing you were here,
 now I'm sitting here trying to hold back these tears.
You're more than an uncle and more then a friend
 I'm loving you always till the very end.

Nightmare of Love

By Breelyn Afusia

Clash, boom, bang goes the anger in my house
My sister with my brother and mom with her spouse
Yelling back and forth, I just can't stand
I sit in a corner, crying while clasping my hands
Wait, it stops, there is silence in the den
But over and over they start fighting again
They love each other really but just don't show it
'Cause one is silent as a rock and the other just a fit
Bullets flying… getting dodged one by one
Having this in life just isn't fun
School, I am safe from anger and frustration
But when I step through that door, words are lost in translation
Shouting, crying and just need to scream
But alas for it was all but a dream
Or so it may seem

DAD

By Andie Melton

Pain and lies are all you have to give
You've hurt me so much
I wish you didn't live

I've cried a million tears
Now I'm ready to stop
Move on with my life and reach the top

I'm going to prove that I didn't need you
Don't bother fighting back because you know it's true
I can't say goodbye because you'll always be there
But deep in my heart I know you don't care

The pain you give me is like and endless river
It doesn't stop flowing
It's sad that that's what keeps you going

I wish weren't part f me because the way
You make me feel inside
That's a feeling I can't hide
Now this is a feeling I must confess
I hat that you've made me so sad
I'm sorry I have to cal you dad

A World Alone

By Dominique Profit

No dad and no mother
Abandoned a baby raised in hell
Being arrested, molested, and beaten
Forced to sling drugs just to put
Food on the table
You want to believe what I hold inside
Can't talk to anybody
Afraid that they will laugh or joke
Instead I write myself a little note
Feeling like everyday I have to fight
Fight for peace, fight for love
And fight for freedom
Being the best I can
But people just don't understand
Being shot at for wearing a certain color
Or being a certain race
People killing for food and things they
Feel are right
Open your eyes it's right in front of you
It's me against the world
Raising me dead sisters baby
Is not so easy
What will I tell him when he gets older
I don't want him to be confused like me
I don't want him to be stuck in
A world alone
Is this how god blessed me?

Up's and Down's

By Daisy Gomez

My life is a bunch of ups and downs,
But mostly downs never ups,
My life is awesome when I am with my friends
My life is horrible when I am at home,
Getting screamed at is an everyday,
Needing help is an all the time,
Getting home is when I starts,
But when I need to talk,
I know I have my two best friends,
But when I don't,
I write it down,
But the only thing that keeps me up,
Are my friends,
I have problems,
That's who I am!

Why

By Kalien Nichols

I often ask myself why?
Why do I care about you?
Why do I confuse what's true?
Why would I lie for you?
And why the hell would I die for you?

I wonder would you do the same for me?
Why would you even care if there's a "we"?
Why don't you just be straight up and honest?
Why do you put on that modest act?
How can I make up for what you lack?

So sorry if there's even an "us"
Would there be faith and trust?
Can we have more just lust?
Why do I bother with you?
Uhhg I hate your crappy moods!

But yet I'm still here
I lie to myself because I'm afraid to
Face my fears. That one day I'll wake up
And you'll be gone. And I my friend
Will be all alone left with all the
Memories that are in my head.
Some way, some how trying to bring back
The dead.

These are questions that have not yet been answered
So now what?
Do I transfer all my emotions to the grass,
As I'm sitting here reminiscing about the past

Young'n Blues

By Kalien Nichols

Once upon a time in a place very close called the city of Cabbage. There were two friends named Eduardo and Kayleena who met each other through a girl named S. Ray. They all became close friends, but one day Kayleena developed more and more feelings for Eduardo, and for a while he felt the same but those feeling died out.

So Kayleena developed a symptom called the young'n blues yall. It hurt and still hurts her to be his friend. She goes out of her way to please him some times she thinks it's all for nothing.

She learned her lesson about Eduardo the hard way, I mean they are still close friends, and she loves him dearly but her feelings are starting to fade.

So the moral is don't try to please everyone and that if it's meant to be than it's meant to be. Kayleena's symptoms to the young'n blues aren't as bad as they use to be, but she's coping and moving forward.

THINK ABOUT LIFE

By Anthony Aranda

So what's happening in your
Would friend are you thriving or
Diving. Does it snow or are
You slow. So you smoke and choke
To fly or can you relate to a
Natural high free as a bird
Or under cover like a nerd
Going around and around out
Of bounds like a Mary go round
Strange and deranged. Do you
Go with the flow like a summer
Breeze cool and at ease
Dreams of bright colored rainbows
Hills of green streams of clear
Blue not a fool speeding on the
River of no return mind bent out
Of line wasting time forget not
My name friend.

ALAYSIA

BY ALIYAH SOUDER

When she was six years old, just a little girl, she was alone on the street. No food, no home, no money. She did not go to school or know how to read. She was just an abandoned small child who carried a heavy backpack on her shoulders. When people saw her, no one questioned her. They knew that her father had left her. Everyone knew everyone's business. Even though no one bothered to help this little girl, she survived on her own. She used public restrooms to wash up and sleep. She waited and waited for someone to help her. One day late at night, someone found her. But it was not family. It happened to be a policeman who was very concerned. The police officer seemed very large to her. He was big and tall. He took her to the station and called child services. When he questioned her, all she could was tell him her name, age, and what happened to her. "My name is Alaysia. I am six. I got in trouble and had to leave and be all alone." Eventually at age eight Alaysia was placed in an adoption home with many other kids and was going to school. She was learning to read and write, she practiced all the time. At school she chose to be alone. She wanted to stay away because even at her young age she could not trust anyone. The kids made fun of her because she didn't speak, and she was not as smart as the other kids. When she was ten, she was finally adopted. Alaysia had a nice family now. A mother, a father, and a caring big brother who was a year older than her. She was now doing well in school had street smarts and wasn't afraid to have friends anymore. Even though she was brave, girls picked on her, and she even got in a physical altercation with one of them. She was suspended and sent home. She never got in trouble with her new parents because they understood her. They had once been adopted too. Her big brother was also adopted. They might have lived in a bad neighborhood, but it felt like heaven to her. The gunshots, the drugs, and violence was just like her old community, so she was used to this. When she was fourteen, she had a nice guy she had been dating, a best friend and her life was going good. On a Saturday, her first date, she was walking out ready to go. Then pop, pop, pop, pop. She was shot and killed. A hard life she lived. She was a wonderful girl who just had hard times.

If Only She Knew

By Lyiasha Gaines

She packed her bags, walked out the door and began walking. Little did she know, she was being watched. She made her way down the sidewalk, no company but the night. Little did she know, she was being watched. The sound of flickering street lights above her head provided an audible burst of reality. Little did she know, she was being watched. As she walked, time and distance became impossible to measure. She didn't know where she was nor did she care. Little did she know, she was being watched. Before she could react, he kicked her down, snatched her bag and walked away. Only if she knew she was being watched. Her attacker continued down the side walk feeling victorious. Little did he know, he was being watched . . .

Little Anya

By Chelsea Salonga

Once there was a young girl named Anya. She was your typical teen, living life as it was, and she just didn't care what happened in the world. Anya was pretty close to her mother, the only person she could always turn to. All that changed when her mother died in a car accident. This affected Anya negatively. Her mother was the only person she really cared about. She would cry her tears out every night and think about why all this happened to her. Soon Anya realized that there's no point in crying anymore because she realized something. She wondered how it felt for her mother to raise her as a single parent. It must have been hard and difficult. Anya started to realize that her mother put her as her top priority. Her mother always did her best just to make her happy, but since she died, Anya turned the tables. Anya was going to make her mother her first top priority and would do whatever it took to make her happy. Anya knows there are ups and downs in life, but there's always going to be a point when you have to move on.

Repercussions

By Brian Amos

Something interesting that happened in my life happened on July 4, the first day of summer. It all started on an early Saturday morning when my parents went out to spend a day together. While my parents were out, my best friend Blake came over on his dirt bike and said, "Hey, Brian, go get your bike and lets go around the block a couple of times." So with my parents gone, I said okay, knowing I was not supposed to be on my bike without permission, but I went out anyway. We set out riding around our neighborhood having a good time, and Blake gets a call from a good friend of both of ours, Noel. Noel said he could hear us riding our bikes and that he was on his way to join us. Blake and I continued around the block until Noel arrived. When Noel arrived, Blake and I were pretty tired of circling around the neighborhood. So Blake, Noel, and I all decided to take our bikes around the corner to Victor Park.

At this point we all arrived to the park and loved the terrain's small jumps, lots of dirt, and plentiful grass. So before we took off and started riding, we always check out the terrain for unsafe things such as pot holes, ditches and unsafe dirt. As always we did that, but without saying anything, I noticed the grass was wet but didn't really worry about it, which was a huge mistake on my behalf. So now every one is having a good time at the park having no clue trouble was on the way. Blake, Noel, and I all started a race down a very long strip of grass about one mile long. As we began to reach the end of the park, I realized I was going 80 mph straight towards a huge tree. So as any other person would, I tried yell to my left where Noel was to tell him to slow down so that I could merge in front of him, but the sounds of our loud motors overpowered my voice. So finally giving up on yelling at Noel, I slammed on the brakes as hard as I could, but slamming on the brakes in wet grass will not bring you to

172

a complete stop right away; you will slide for a long period of time like I did.

So now sliding towards a huge tree I had a million thoughts going through my head: should I jump, should I stay, should I throw the bike, should I fall with the bike? Getting closer and closer, I had no choice but to stay on the bike. At this point I'm now laying on my back looking at Blake and Noel. By the way their facial expressions were, I knew this was serious. While Blake was trying to keep me calm and Noel was calling on an ambulance, all I could think about was the punishment I was going to be given. It seemed that it took the ambulance hours to come, but when it did, I was thankful. Soon after they put me in the back of the van, I could feel the cool, fresh A.C. cut off, realizing the van had stopped. Now we were at Harbor UCLA where they rushed me straight to the ER to treat me. The doctors had me on so many meds I couldn't feel my legs. Laying in the ER was so peaceful until suddenly it thought I heard my dad's voice. I became scared that I was going to be in trouble, but luckily I wasn't. Now being up and alert, I explained the story to my dad, and soon after I was done telling him the story, the doctor walked in to inform me of my injuries. Come to find out, I broke my thigh bones and had to have surgery to have them fixed.

From this accident I learned a number of things. For example, I learned that if I notice something my friends don't know no matter how little it is, I need to make sure they are aware of it. Another thing I learned was even if your parents aren't watching, you still should do the right thing

UNTITLED

By Anonymous

There was once a girl who was very beautiful. Guys everywhere adored her, and she was loved everywhere she went. But this girl only had eyes for one person, a guy who claimed to love her more then any other person. So over time the two became very close and fell in love. At the height of their love came another girl who wanted to hurt their relationship. The more the beautiful girl loved her boyfriend, her affections seemed different. He only took notice of the other girl. The beautiful girl grew tired of having her heart twisted and tormented. Why was she trying to please this guy so much? Who knows, but one night she grew sick of it. So the next day as her boyfriend walked with the other girl, she looked at the two of them and decided to just let go. She followed her inconsiderate boyfriend as he walked with her and realized that they look good together. The beautiful girl decided to be the bigger person. She reached into her bag, took a knife, and solved her problem. She killed both her boyfriend and the other girl so they could be happy together in heaven forever. The beautiful girl no longer had to vie for his affection, and the beautiful girl lived happily ever after.

Graduation from Middle School

By Alejandra Delgado

An important event from my life was when I graduated from Stephen White Middle School. I graduated on June 19, 2008, when I was 14 years old. This was an important event in my life because on that day my family went to my school to see me walk the stage, and it was unforgettable.

When I found out that I was going to graduate from Stephen White, I was excited and proud of myself. I had been waiting for that moment since sixth grade. When I went home that evening, I told my parents the news. They were very proud of me and told me that I deserved it.

On the hot evening of June 19, 2008, I was really excited . Everyone waited in their chairs in the hot sun, parents holding gifts they had brought-- balloons, flowers, candy, necklaces, and other goodies—for their graduates. I remember receiving a lot of laces and candy necklaces. Every parent waited anxiously for their children to be announced, and they would scream and clap loudly when they heard their own child's name.

When it was my turn, I nervously started to climb the stairs and walk carefully across the stage. This was because I had high heels on. As I shook the principal's hand and in the other hand received my diploma, everybody started to clap, but most especially it was my parents, aunt, and uncles. When I went back to my seat I felt really happy!

After the whole thing was over, my whole family took pictures of me with my cousin who had graduated with me. We took a lot of pictures. After this we went to a Mexican restaurant and ate very good food. I had a very good day on my graduation. At the restaurant, I saw that I had gotten a huge sunburn on my arms and my back. It hurt, but it didn't affect how proud I felt. This would be a day that I will never forget.

SILENCE IS SCREAMING

BY GEENA DASHIELL

When eyes are closed and daydreaming,
They appear open and attentive.
These eyes dream of fantasies and truth
Instead of seeing lies and reality.

Ears seem to listen to daily noise
But the thoughts turn into music that clouds the ears.
They hear the words unspoken
And the thoughts of others.

This mouth can speak thoroughly,
But communicates poorly.
The tongue holds back what the mouth can't say.
The mouth has been commanded, and it must obey.

These hands hold what they're never held.
They hold the weights of others.
They write the truths that the mouth cannot speak.

In silence, you can hear what's not being said.
The hands write these words, screaming,
"Please hold these hands!"
Music in my ears, singing,
"Please listen!"
The eyes open, willing.
"Please look at me!"
Mouth shut tight. Silence.

WALK IN MY SHOES

By Rolini Matua

Walk in my shoes
And you will see
How tough it is to be like me.
Running away from all the pain, no love,
No care, no hope to gain.
Waiting and waiting for happiness to come,
There's no excitement, there's no fun.

Walk in my shoes
And see what I do
From feeling good to feeling to feeling blue,
From old days becoming new,
From following footsteps or having a chance to choose.
Just being myself is hard to do.
From having to go through stuff I never been through,
To being alone and having no clue.

Walk in my shoes
And have a great time
From paying for stuff, not even spending a dime.
From doing good to doing bad,
From feeling happy to feeling sad.
From getting in trouble for the things I did not do
From helping others to do what they do.

Walk in my shoes
And feel real sad feel, real happy
Or feel real mad.
Feel real glad or feel real sorry;
Don't feel ashamed; don't feel worried.

Walk in my shoes
And you will see how different it is to be like me.
I'm not like you, you're not like me
We might be different in ways I can't see.

Walk in my shoes
And you will see how I am and how I might be.
Being me is what I do.
Sometimes I feel old, sometimes I feel new.
Sometimes it's easy to be myself.
So if you're done with my shoes
Please put them on the shelf.

Sports Education, Recreation and Fitness (SERF)

Lead Teacher: Mr. Labasan
Participating Teacher: Ms. Kol

BASKETBALL

By Curtis Moore

Basketball is my goal;
I loved it since I was 4
I watch the games to see the famous,
But most of the time they're just shameless.
I watch them shake and fake,
But most of the time they don't make shots.
I love basketball because I love the game
And I want people to remember my name.
My shot is a little wack, that's a fact,
But I will change so I don't end up like Shaq.

I AM SO FLY

By Robert Guinmary

I am so fly like a bird in the sky
I am so fly till I die
I am so fly read my rhyme
Take your time
I am so fly as I make this beat
Get out your seat
Cause tonight we're going to cuddle in the sheets
Cheese and fleas, bumble bees
Look at me and freeze
Just like Steve and me!!!

GONE

By Evelyn Gonzales

First Love,
Just felt so right.
Unstoppable,,
Was how I felt
I held nothing back.
I fell quick for you.
But not once did you tell me,
You loved me.
Till I was gone!
Thinking I was just another girl
But feeling I was something else.

Poem #2

By Joel Ambriz

The weekends are a time to relax
Were we can hang out with friends
We have fun without the worry of school
Two days of freedom is what I need.
The weekends are very very cool
On the weekend ill have no need
And I wont have no rules
The weekends are almost here
Kicking it on the pool with nothing to ruin it.
Its very near
The weekend is now here.

Poem #2

By Chauncey Cunningham

Life is an elevator,
There are 2 paths to choose from,
You can go up or down,
Sometimes you may have to climb,
Sometimes you may have to sigh,
And when you look up you see the end of the elevator
Hear it comes the end of he life long tour,
Today is the day that your mother pray,
But now I can see,
The end is here.

You were the one

By Karysa Greene

You were the one
That said you loved me
How can you just let us scatter
Yu are for me and I am for you
We were forever no matter what we do
But you were the one who walked away
And that told me you didn't need me
So don't let me be he one you miss
Decided to leave me
You were the one that said we would last
Forever no matter what came between us
You were the one who said you would love
Me forever
You were the one that walked out
YOU WERE THE ONE!!!

DREAM AT THE BEACH

By Vanessa Villanueva

There I was walking at the beach
With the perfect guy
His hair black like chocolate
And his eyes blue as the sea.
There we were walking at the tanish sea.
Barefooted,
Watching the sunset,
Hand in hand,
Talking bout life,
Until the big dark wave took him away
Waking up from my dream
In my dirty blue room.

FOOTBALL

By Cheyenne Sagiao

Football is a sport I like best,
The end zone are posted to the east and to the west.
Hitting and smashing is hat I love bout the game.
When its done, all would have heard my name.
I especially like to rush the quarterbacks
Each game I try to get at least 3 to 4 sacks.
Defensive or offensive line is where I start.
On the field its no joke, you play hard you got to have heart.
I can hear the support "we want a touchdown, a touchdown!"
I always play to win, high school is not the end,
I AM COLLEGE BOUND!

POEM #3

By Zeke Torres

The waterfalls,
as the bear stands tall,
Grizzly's growling ,
As the fish is scowling,
The waters wet,
As the fish leaps into the sky,
The taste of pure blood,
Dripping out the bears mouth,
The smell f wild life,
Is in the sky,
The mater is still tall,
But the bear is not so tall.

POEM #2

By Rose Medina

Everyday we have to go to school.
We wake up bright and early.
Ring! Ring! Ring! The bell rings.
We have to be in class before seven forty-two am.
Sometimes we have to hear are annoying teachers all day.
Some teachers start to annoy you or some are always on you back.
We get lots of homework and class work.
We always have those difficult test or those pop quizzes,
Where in class for two hole long hours.
The classes at school are golf boring.

POEM #1

BY CEZIKA CONCHA

I'm sitting waiting, wishing,
Hoping for a poem to come to mind.
Yet no subject or though appears,
Who knew writing a poem was hard,
I stare at a blank paper,
And stare out into an empty space.
Time seems to be passing by,
Who knew writing a poem was hard.
Now I sit here, expressing my thoughts,
Just wanting to finish this assignment.
At first I though it would be easy, but
Who knew writing a poem was hard.

Life

By Dionicio Moreno

Life comes at you fast
But sometimes it can be a blast
At times you may feel down
But you must never frown
Life comes at you fast
Don't let one minute of it past
Go out and enjoy yourself
Don't sit there like a doll on a shelf
Life is like a box of chocolates
You never know what you are going to get

∞

A tiny heart-beat

By Linda Pendelonzo

A life that's given birth to,
A life that's growing strong,
A way to find the strength,
To keep going on and on.
How can something so beautiful be taken away,
The tiny heart-beat flutters within her womb,
Causing my love to sway.
To go back to what once had been
With sorrow in every word,
To be forgiven again.

BARREN DESERT

By Jeremiah Fuller

Alone in a barren desert
Alone the cactus stands
By itself on a lonely night
The elements in fights
For its right
To survive
Sharp long weapon
Protect its fleshy watery soul
As if his life depends on it
Alone in a barren desert
We each stand.

Poem #2

By Gregory Lemelin

High school can be rough at times.
Which makes me even tough at times.
Sometimes it can be tiring.
Sometimes it can be inspiring.
The homework, reports, quizzes and test are
All part of the stress.
It's a challenge I admit but I have promised to commit.
Never say I cant and never say I wont.
I must focus on each day,
So I can pass and get
Good grades.
Try to do my best on each and every test.
This is what will lead me to the path of success.

∞

Poem # 1 School

By Edgar Rubio

In school you have to be cool
If you act a fool you might get schooled
Teacher and students never getting along
But when they do they make a real good crew
So don't act a fool you school know what to do
When its comes to school be like me try to do all the work
Sometimes working out to the ladies.
That don't want me but its all good.

LIFE

By Cimon Crisostomo

Life is here
Life is there
Life is circle
Life is square
From the positive and negatives,
In life as a whole
You either take it all in.
Or flush it all down a bowl.
From leaving or being left behind
All those memories stay in your mind
Closing and opening a new chapter in life.
Hit me up and get in line
Life is o valuable to just sit and watch time fly,
Because you never know when it's your turn to die.

I HAD A CHANCE

By Michelle Oropeza

I had a chance to say I love you
I had a chance to have you around my arms
I have a chance to be with you on the phone until 3 o clock in the
morning
I had a chance to buy you gifts that you would always love
I had a chance to tell everybody that I was with you and see there
jealous face they would make
But no…
I didn't get that chance
I didn't get that chance because
I tried too hard to get that chance
I tried too hard!
And I regret it, now
I lost that chance.
If I could go back I would try to just be myself
I hope I get another chance.

Technology Education Knowledge Prep
(TEK Prep)

Lead Teacher: Mr. Nash
Participating Teachers: Ms. Ni & Ms. Bird

Science Teacher

By Ricardo Arambula

Vesuvius forever damaged the land.
Ominous standing tall over Pompeii
Latent were the forces that built inside
Catastrophic was its destruction in its wake
Apocalyptic view of its rage
New life springs up as peace returns
Onwards forever the time flows giving new birth to the scorched
land

∞

By Aaron Carranza

Large traces of rock, mud, and water
A powerful and devastating force
Having broken many a landscape
Arriving to far-off lands
Restless and relentless flow

By Aaron Carranza

Marvelous red glow in the dark
A liquid flame
Greedy for land
Moving and carving a burning path
Astonishing life in the end

∞

By Karla Camarena

Restoration of the island seems impossible.
At one time the island was a…
Paradise thriving,
And fertile.
New to the land Polynesians were;
Unbalanced, the land became
Impossible for restoration.

By Antonio Cruz

Destruction of trees
Earth's ill-shaven haircut.
Families take all that animals hold.
Over time, the lush green turns to light brown.
Resurrection of life is futile.
Everyone leaves the barren desert.
Sand tears the flesh of all life.
Time to react is NOW.
All life is tough to bring back
Through science we can bring them back.
Is all this work worth a simple mistake?
Our mistake led to an extinction.
Not much more can set-up a chain reaction so destructive.

By Justin Aguilo

State of
Underusing
Substances so
That
All people
In the
Nation can
Always
Believe
In equal
Liberty
In
Total use of substances
Yet, while providing for others as well......

By Linda Penalonzo

Intended to measure and
Navigate operations.
Dedication of a substance
Independent of other physical systems.
Condition of the environment
Accurate information
Take a reaction
Oppose the nature
Retract to connection
Statistics of nature

By Autumn Burrell

Emotional impact through your eyes.
Community
Over all respect to the world.
Love and care for your wonderful Earth.
One chance to change-
Giving back what has been given to you.
I am my own impact.
Closer to your home;
Analyzing your progress;
Living the way you SHOULD.

Forgetting the past to protect the future.
Oxygen in Earth is one true nature.
Over coming fear that you see tomorrow,
Touching ones heart with your will to survive.
Passion for living life the right way.
Racing for Earth's true beauty.
Indicate your level of Earth's destruction.
Never giving up on your BACKYARD!
Trust, that change will come.

By Kendrick Mendoza

Saving more and using less
Understanding ways of living
Saving more usage in the environment
Teaching
Amount
Inhabitable life
New ideas
Acomplishing a task
Balance
Information
Limited needs
Ideas
Thinking about what to do
YOU using less materials.

By Michelle Ponce

Research of the land showed
An island paradise uninhabitated.
Polynesians brought poison
And eventually they forced a way of life upon the island.
Not for long the island remained.
Use of resources, which have gone dry
In the island erosion reeks havoc.

By Victor Iniguez

Excessive use of
Carbon dioxide and
Other materials needed to
Live without limiting
Ourselves.
Growing and making the materials
Is sometimes hard to
Complete.
All the sturff we buy
Later ends up as trash.

For some
Of us that is not a problem, but
Others buy and buy.
That is a habit we need to stop. So
Please think of what we need
Really to survive
In life. We do not
Need all the iPods and
The nice clothes, those are our wants.

By Mariel Dennis

Destruction of nature is
Especially evil and all those
Ferocious chainsaws
Oppose this immoral act and
Regain your forrest back.
Earn your chances by
Saving trees
Treat nature with respect
And care
The choice is yours.
It's either now,
Or
Never.

CITY

By Emmanuel Rebollar

The business building is like the chief of a tribe.
The business building is what is in charge of people's lives.
The business building smiles when its employees do their work.

The restaurants are like the legend on a map.
The restaurants give me advice.
The restaurants never yell when the jib goes wrong.

The parks are like a paradise of life's joy.
The parks are what bring me entertainment.
The parks cry when I cry from sorrow.

The hospital is like gives me my strength.
The hospital always gives me aid in times of need.
The hospital allows me to heal.

The hotels are like the fingers that stick together.
The hotels are the left and right hand of a mother.
The hotels listen to each other no matter what.

The streets are like lava flowing and destroying homes.
The streets are what cause horrible disasters.
The streets laugh when innocent birds die.

My Family is Like the Earth

By Mariel Dennis

My grandma is the core,
The heart of the earth.
It holds the family together.
The sun is my mom,
Through her light she guides he children.
The trees are like my father,
Providing food and shelter.
My siblings and I are the flowers of the earth,
The beauty of our parents' world.
My cousins are the monkeys of the jungle.
The monkeys love to eat, talk, and play,
No matter what season or day.
The things of the planet work together
Building one earth.
Without the sun, there are no trees
Without trees, there are no monkeys
Without flowers, there is no beauty
Without the core, there is no bond
Without my earth, I am nothing.

Poem

By Efrain Ornelas

Like the frame, my dad
protects us.
Like the tires, my mom
guides us.
Like the seats, my sisters
bare within.
I am the engine that fills
my family with life
and smiles.
My family's like a car,
working together to keep each other
moving forward.
I am a battery energizing
my surroundings.
The tires are my insurance,
gripping the road with
their rubbery hands.
My life, my family, we
are a car.

Family is Like a House

By Cassie Player

A house needs walls, a roof, floors
A fence, paint, and of course, a door.
A mother is like the walls,
Walls make sure everything is stable.
A father is like the roof,
The roof protects and shields everything.
A sister is like the floor,
The floor keeps you standing tall.
A brother is like the fence,
A fence makes sure nobody will come in and
Hurt or break the string structure.
The youngest child is like paint.
Like paint, it hides any scuff marks,
Or hurt, and makes everything seem great.
Nieces and nephews are the doors
Because without doors, you wouldn't feel
Welcome.

T. V.

By Iomari Sanares

I talk and I am used for entertainment,
I create pictures and I am often stored in the basement.
I can teach you about the sea.
I will tell you what to do when you get stung by a bee.
I am the best invention and I am a T.V.

Family

By Cesar Badillo

Have you ever wondered
What hold a book together
For years so that it doesn't break apart?

If my family was a book,
Then my dad would be the outside covers.
He is the covers,
Like an umbrella,
Keeping the book safe from the rain.

My mom is like the table of contents.
She knows where everything is,
And she has everything organized.

My brother is like the index.
Sometimes he is useful,
But other times
He is not.

I would say that I am
The pages.
I am full of knowledge and questions at the same time
But the pages are always talking,
Always staring at you while you stare back

Untitled

By Autumn Burrell

My hole will tell it all
The beat keeps the melody and voice so strong
1
2
3
4
The knocking of the Beat scares my head
From my body to my back
The Back is the most important
as
A
Matter of
F
A
C
T
Back is beautiful
The Back is Love
The ukulele needs
Strings, chords, pegs,
a body, neck, head,
beat, melody, voice,
The hole and Love
My ukulele is like a sunset
It brings joy, pain, and tears to me
I am the ukulele, I am everything
Autumn
Jae
Burrell.

The Band

By Megan Pinzon

The trumpet so loud and fierce that his
noise can pierce
like an aggravated father that condemns the foolish
He loudly sings in a deep voice, he is the noise you
can't control, so behold
The mother that takes care of the melodies
like a bass after the guitar that gently sings
She'll make you depressed with her vibrant notes
She is the notes that play throughout the song
so sing along
The bashing beats that make you feel
I'm like the drum, the real deal!
I'm the chosen one that brings it all together
I'm the drum that makes you sore, never!
As all of us unite tonight
We will make you dance
Because we rock out just right

I Can't Stand It

By Kimberly Arana

I can't stand it
His face
His eyes
Just plain HIM
Staring at me
I can't stand it
What we had
What I thought we had
I was betrayed
The way things happened
So hard to have it sink in
I can't stand it
The way you were
I saw it coming
But I didn't believe
I can't stand it
The way I was
When the break up happened
And that sweet smell of relief
I can't stand it

Snake

By Mitchell Capulong

I feel the sting of a snake
Not so fun indeed
To see it is funny
To feel it is not
As I tried to tame him, I thought
Sweet
Until I noticed I was just the same
He bit me not so kindly
To think I was related to him
His stupidity led to my downfall
As I feel the sting of a snake

GRANDMA

BY MICHAEL TRIPLETT

My grandma Stella had the greatest impact on my life. She was small but she had the biggest heart that I have ever seen.

I walked into the kitchen following the sweet scent of waffles and pork links. Grandma told me, "Good morning miho. Did you sleep well last night?" "Yes, I did," I replied with a smile. Then Grandma said, "That's good. Here's your breakfast." She handed me a plate with pork links and waffles and a glass of milk. I sat down and ate my breakfast.

In the afternoon, I went in the kitchen and found my grandma making dinner. She put the food in the oven, after that I grabbed her hand and we started dancing like we always would when she would cook. She told me, "You're going to have all the girls dancing with you when you're older." I said, "No, grandma because I only like dancing with you." Then she started to laugh and said, "Thank you, but I just want o dance with you." She started laughing. I knew she was laughing because she felt special.

Early Saturday morning, I got up to watch T.V. as I normally did. My mom rented Pokémon 2000 so I put it on. My grandma sat on the table drinking her coffee, and we watched the movie together. In one scene in the movie a character said, "Don't talk that way about the opposite sex." I didn't understand what she meant so I asked grandma, "What does the opposite sex mean?" She said, "It means that I'm a girl and you're a boy. It's just telling you that boys and girls are different." I said, "Thanks grandma I kind of get it." After that talk we just finished watching the movie.

It was around noon, and I just got out of school. My grandma picked me up, and asked, "Since you didn't stay and eat lunch at school, do you want to eat?" I said, "Yes." I knew my grandma would take me to Burger King like she always did. It would be our little getaway from my brother and sister. We went to Burger King and ate there, and went home. Later, we went to pick up my brother and sister from school. While we were waiting in the car, I grabbed the air freshener and sprayed it. I looked at the top like a retard and sprayed it in my eyes.

Grandma started getting sick and was in and out of the hospital a few times. She got really sick and as sent to the hospital in Down Town LA. My mom, Koral, Rodger, Grandpa, and I went up to see her a lot when she was there, because she as so far from home. She ended up being sent back to Torrance Memorial Hospital. A while after she was there, the doctors knew she was going to die, so we had a hospital bed set up at the house for her to come home. The doctors brought grandma home and put her in the bed. I couldn't stand to see her sick, so I stayed out of the living room as much as possible.

I got home from school and saw grandma in her hospital bed. I wanted to watch T.V. but we had guests over to see her, so I went into my mom's room. I turned on the T.V. and did my homework. It was about four thirty when my mom came in the room crying. She told me, "Grandma's no longer with us." I didn't know what she meant, so I asked, "She went back to the hospital?" Mom gave me a hug and said, "No, she passed away." At that moment I froze as my heart broke into what felt like a million pieces. No, I couldn't believe it. Someone who had been there all that time, had died. I began crying in my mom's arms. She comforted me by telling me, "Grandma is in a better place now. She isn't going to be in anymore pain." I stayed in my mom's room for a while until she came and took me to my aunt's house so I wouldn't be able to see the people take my grandma away.

Two Brothers

By Paolo Manay

Muscular, fit, talented and annoying. My little brother Noel, the boy who is the total opposite of me. He's a bee buzzing over my head. He's more muscular than me yet, I still have more power. He is physically fit, but I still top him off with strength and speed. In sports like basketball he beats me in skills, but at times I would play much better than him. As I said before he's my opposite, he has the physical talent while I have the brains. Though at ties I envy, but in the end I'm proud of him.

I have many good memories with my little brother for example; it was the day that my little brother and I were going to meet my cousin Robbie. We were not really excited, because we barely knew him, but he was really nice to us. When we saw Robbie, Noel asked me, "Kinsa ba na", then I said, "atong igagaw." The only English word we said to him was, "Hi," because that's the only English word my brother and I knew. After we all introduced each other, my uncle told us that we were going to the beach. All of us little kids shouted."Yay," out of excitement. So we all went to the car to begin our trip to the beach. On the way, Robbie, Noel, my cousin Ryan and I were singing and stuff. When we got there, the water was still like a Buddhist monk, meditating. We swam, played around, and played with water guns. After that day, my little brother and I have not seen Robbie since.

March 19, 2009 was one of the days I shined in basketball. While my little brother was hesitating, I was showing off how my skills improved. Noel was playing poorly. I had to take risky measures to win, like getting the rebound and almost twisting my ankle. I went against semi-skilled players, so I learned a lot. Noel always tells me to go against people who are better to get better. Noel looked pathetic, but I encouraged him to step up his game. Then in the next two games, he improved his game and his aggression. Without hesitation we beat the other team with pare Manay bro's teamwork.

Something my little brother and I have a lot in common is video games. W would always spend a lot of time playing "Dynasty Warriors Xtreme Legends." W would always try to get our own kingdom, but it gets very complicated because he always dies in the end. At times, we would go to my friend Gerard's house to play Halo 3 on left or dead. In coop games, Gerard, Noel and I are good at team work. But at times when we are playing Halo 3, I get sent to another team and then my team ends up winning because of me. But Noel is still better in video games than me, even though I own him at times. He's one of my greatest rivals in video games and other tuff.

Though we have a lot of differences, we get along just fine. Even though we annoy each other or get into loud arguments or as we call it, "intense debates," he's one of the people who influence me. And even though I'm envious of him for having the good physical qualities, I respect him, love him, and I am proud to have him in my life.

The Pain of One Family

By Donnalyn Montojo

It was one of the days when things are least expected - August 24, 2006. It was two days after my birthday when my mom took my dad to the doctor's for a check up. He had gout at the time. When they came home, my mom took my dad directly to their room, told him to rest and go to sleep. My mom left for work, so I went into to the room where my dad was as to check how he was doing. I asked him if he took his medicine for gout and for his high blood pressure. He said, "Yes. Anak matutulog muna ako." I said, "Sige po," and lay next to him for at least ten minutes.

When I went back inside the room to check on how he was doing, my dad was soaking wet with sweat, which was really unusual because it wasn't hot. The fan was right in front of him and he had a t-shirt over his chest full of sweat. When I was waking him up he wasn't as alert as usual. It took him at least two minutes to wake up. I told him to get up so he could change his t-shirt and I was going to get him some water. That's when things started to feel different. When I was coming back with the cup of cold water, in the corner of my eye I saw my dad fall. It was like a hungry seagull catching its food because the moment passed so quickly. I then started to panic and called my brothers to help my dad get up, but he became heavier. He couldn't even get himself up.

When my dad started to speak, he was asking for a bucket in a slurred tone. It was a baby talking and we couldn't understand a word. I called my mom and told her that something was wrong with Daddy. When mom said she wanted to speak with Daddy, I gave the phone to him. All my dad said was the name they call each other, "Love," and that was the last word we all heard from him. When I took the phone away my mom said to call 911. After I hung up the phone, I dialed 911

When the first ring rang, my heart was pounding really fast like a girl in love without a happy ending. As the operator said, "911, what's your emergency?" I told the voice on the other end that something was wrong with my dad. She started to ask questions like if he's bleeding, sweating, etc. After I said that he's really sweating and he can't get up, she told me that the ambulance will be there in about 45 seconds to a minute. As I heard the ambulance coming, its sound started to tell me that my dad was coming with it. When the firefighters and paramedics came in they went to my dad's room and checked on him. As they were examining him, they started to tell him that he had a mild stroke due to his blood pressure. His blood pressure was 217 over 218. That's when I felt like I had an F on the biggest test of the year.

When the paramedics told us to follow them to Long Beach Memorial Hospital, I started to cry because I knew at that moment something was really wrong. When they took my dad into the emergency room, a doctor came out and asked me, my two brothers, and my uncle to into a private room. He told us that my dad took a cetacean test and a hemorrhage bigger than his first was found. I was really confused because I didn't know what a hemorrhage was at the time, and all I understood is that he needed to have brain surgery.

Five minutes after my mom came, we heard a woman's voice over the speaker's, "Will the family of Donald Ramos please proceed to the desk." As we approached the desk a doctor in a surgeon's uniform asked, "Are you the Ramos family?" My mom replied, "Yes," in a very sad voice. We followed the doctor and my mom started to feel bad news coming our way. When the doctor told us to wait in the private room, my mom started to freak out. "I don't know what I would do if something happened to your dad!" she started to cry.

The doctor came back in and told us that my dad was in a very critical condition. He had a stroke and an aneurism due to his blood pressure. One of the blood vessels popped in his brain and that caused the hemorrhage. The doctor asked us if we wanted to take the risk of brain surgery. At this point my mom burst into tears. She didn't know what to do. She asked the doctor if she could see my dad, and as much as I wanted to go with her, I was afraid of what I would see. As we called my mom's and dad's siblings, I began to cry harder. I just couldn't understand that I wouldn't have a dad anymore if he didn't survive the operation. When the rest of the relatives came, we cried and prayed together.

Six hours went by in the waiting room, and they were the longest hours of my life. The doctor finally came in and informed us that my dad survived the operation but was still in a critical condition. He also said that we couldn't visit him that night and had to go home so my dad could rest. When we walked out of the hospital my whole family gathered and prayed for my dad's survival.

We had bog financial problems at the time, so later that week we had to move to another house because the owner said we were one month behind on rent. While my dad was in the hospital, we had to quickly find a house we could live in. All of our problems were piling up and they were so difficult that it felt like Einstein himself couldn't figure them out. My mom didn't sleep at all. She was always with my dad, taking care of him. We could understand the situation my mom was in, and at that time, all the attention was on my dad.

I was with my older sister the first time I went to visit him in the ICU. The room was dark and not a single light shone in the dark sky. I looked at him, and he jerked every five seconds as I tried not to cry. When I said, "Daddy, this is Donnalyn," he jerked even faster and his blood pressure began to rise. I told him, "Dad, just relax, we're okay. Magpagaling ka lang ha." I saw a teardrop fall. With all the wires attached to him and the bandage over his head, I couldn't imagine how much pain he was in.

My dad was in ICU for a month and a half before he was moved to Little Company of Mary Institute. That seventh grade year was difficult for me because I had to miss many days of school to help my mom take care of dad. It was a hard but good experience for me because I got to take care of my dad more than ever before. I learned how to change his clothes, change the linens, pull up and change the diaper, give him a bath, and anything else to help him. Sometimes my sister and I would stay there until one or two in the morning to make sure he was comfortable and had everything he needed. The nurses were surprised that a twelve year old girl could learn how to do those things and remember which medicine the nurses needed to give my dad.

He remained at that institute for months, and in May of that year we got a phone call that my dad had a fever of a 100. We called back around 2 am and were informed that he was taken to Torrance Hospital because his fever increased. When we got to the emergency room, my dad did not look well. He was in a critical condition again and was moved to the ICU. As my mom was talking to the nurse outside, I remained in my dad's room with my brother. I said to my dad, "You can do it. It is just like before. Just be okay because you promised me that you're going to teach me how to cook, to drive, to be my first dance on my 18th birthday, and walk me down the aisle when I get married. Right?" I began to cry and asked my dad to give me a kiss. He puckered his lips and I kissed him. That was the last kiss I ever gave my dad.

The next day he was comatose. My mom called y older sister to come see her dad. My sister said, "I don't want to go because I know once I go something bad will happen." My mom again asked her to come. I went with my sister that night to my dad's room. She started to speak and said, "Daddy, I never said this to you but I loved you more than my real dad and I'm lucky that you showed me how to love a dad," and she began to cry. When I looked at my dad, I saw tears coming down his face. I said, "I love you, daddy," and left.

The next morning my mom woke up holding a necklace with my mom's and dad's picture in it. Five minutes later we received a phone call from my aunt saying that my dad passed away. May 30, 2007 was the saddest day of my life and my mom and I cried more than ever before. My dad will live forever in my heart and our memories will last until eternity.

Loss of Fallen Friends

By Antonio Cruz

As I stand on a grave, here are a few questions I must ask you before you can understand the story. What do you do when you see a beloved friend lifeless on the floor? How about watching each one of your friends die one by one? This is what I had to experience from October 17, 2007 to November 3, 2007.

The story begins on September 3, 2007. My seventh grade year was about to begin in just a few days, so my family went shopping for supplies. The Cerritos Mall had a fresh smell like the air after a rainy evening. All the stores had Halloween-themed paraphernalia stuck on their windows – '90s stickers of crappy mummies or dumb-looking vampires. I wondered why they didn't buy some up-to-date stickers instead. We traveled throughout the mall examining the many items in stock while trying to find some materials.

"Okay, so what else do we need?" my mom asked after we checked off the last few things on our list.

"Pencils! We need more pencils!" my little brother yodeled.

"We already have more than enough pencils. We need some erasers, a few folders, and several binders," I said.

We walked to a nearby Staple store to het the materials. As we walked, I thought about a few questions about the next school year: What will the next school year be like? Who will be there and who will be in the other schools? How much homework will I receive each day? How rough will the classes be? These thoughts troubled me the entire day.

As soon as we were done shopping, we started to drive home. The road was a twisting snake slithering along the earth and made me lightheaded.

"Hold on for a little while. I have to make a few errands," my mom said.

"Oh, man. Can you please hurry up? My favorite show will be on in a half hour," my little brother exclaimed.

For almost two whole hours we had to wait for our mother. I was so bored that I had to play "I Spy" with my brother. It felt like an eternity waiting for her. Just when I was about to die from boredom, she finally walked out of the post office.

"What took so long? I missed the new Zack & Cody," my brother complained loudly.

"The line was long and we needed more stamps. You watch too much television anyway," my mom replied. We began to go home, but the drive was so slow that it was like we were riding on top of a snail.

As soon as we got home, my big brother told me news I didn't expect to hear.

"Hey, I have something to tell you. Our dog just had puppies," my big brother told me.

I already knew she was pregnant, but I didn't know when the puppies would come out. I checked inside the doghouse and found five newborn pups scrambling around. This unexpected present would keep my mind off the coming school year.

School would begin the next day, and I didn't know what to do next. I worried about what I had to bring, what I had to wear, and what new or old friends I would shortly meet. As soon as I took a look at the pups, all my worries drowned away.

"Wake up. It's time for school," my mom yelled at daybreak.

"A few more minutes," my little brother whispered.

"Aww! Why now?" my big brother asked.

I didn't want to go to school, but I was required. I went to school as any other normal day.

Two weeks after the first day of school the puppies opened their eyes. The finally took their first view of the world. It felt good knowing that they could finally see my entire family.

Once the pups lived almost a month and I saw how they looked and acted, I named them. Their names were Mini-Me the 2nd, Gaviota, Pearl, Sparkles, and Prissy Jr. Everything was well with them, but they seemed to be too much to take care of. We had to give them to loving families, but only one family that we knew wanted one of the puppies. The puppies gave me relief from my predicaments in my first month of school when the unforeseeable happened.

On October 17, 2007, one of the puppies got a terrible virus. Mini-Me the 2nd got a terrible disease known as the Parboll virus, a virus that destroys the digestive system. On November 3, 2007, after our hard work to make him better, he passed away and infected the others. Each one fell never to wake up. It seems that Death stood next to the doghouse waiting for its prey. Luckily, we were able to give away Sparkles before the virus outbreak.

I never felt the same since. Almost two weeks after the incident I was completely disoriented, but school never waits for anyone. I went to school and many things began to happen. My grades began to slowly decline. I didn't care about my friends. They tried to cheer me up but didn't succeed. I know they tried their best, but it only made things worse. I felt sorrow each day after that event. They only lived for one month and a half! If I could have done something, then they would have been able to lie happy and blissful lives with their loving owners. I know that I couldn't do much, but I am happy to know that at least on of the puppies went to a good family and is currently living a good life.

You probably thought that I lost a human friend, but anyone can be your friend. For me, the puppies were my friends.

THE PROMISED LAND

BY ANTHONY ONG

It was very cold outside of the strange airport. I use the word "strange" because the airport was clean and unusual to me. I was wearing about three layers of clothes but the bitter cold could still reach my unaccustomed skin and make me shiver.

"Naa na ta," said my cousin when my family and I reached the extravagant car. This was the fanciest car I saw since coming out of the enormous airplane. It reminded me of the transportation in Cagayan De Ono, my dear hometown.

"Hoy! Naa na ang jeep! Hali na dinhi Jay!" my father said in haste, took my hands, and entered the vehicle. I was four back then, when we first rode the dirty and crowded vehicle. As the car was started in a smooth motion, I heard the back and forth of tiresome conversations from my cousins and my parents. I was only thinking about the videogames they had in this country and whether they even played fun, interactive games. We finally came to my aunt's spectacular house. The only thing that annoyed me when we went inside was the whining of my demanding three year old brother.

"Kamusta na," said my concerned aunt.

"Okay, lang tita," I replied in a shy voice. The only thing that made me why was the fact that I didn't feel like her "darling" nephew since she was my step-mother's sister.

Dinner was great and typical for Filipinos in this country since they still use rice as a main dish. Although I never knew that meat tasted really different depending on the country you're in, it reminded me of a day I never wanted to remember.

"Kaon na Jay," my father told me in a tired voice while he set up the table. I walked to the dinner table and prayed before eating the food since it's a tradition fir my family to do so. I loved the food, but it tasted weird and a bit raw.

"Kanding ma na doy," my father told me while he laughed at me. I didn't really mind eating goat but the way he cooked it made it taste strange. I almost wanted to throw up, so I stopped eating it. Although I was still hungry, I left the dinner table to watch television.

Sleeping was as hard as being in that huge and fancy airplane. It might have been jetlag, but I could already hear my father snoring from the other guestroom. I wondered what to expect from this country and thought to at least be good in school to be successful and make my father proud. I thought I would have a great morning tomorrow.

The harsh morning was like the night we came, but I actually loved the greasy bacon here since it was expensive in the Philippines. The cheapest thing you could eat there was a stray dog walking in a dirty and dark alley. I never tried one because my father didn't want me to eat something filthy like that even though we lived in poverty after my mother left us.

My amazing father lived in a crowded family of twelve. His family struggled since his parents relied financially only on an old and dusty restaurant that mad just enough money to feed them. My careless father was a brilliant guy but made the wrong choices. He ditched school to go watch a movie or do anything else he wanted. Even his teacher told him that he was very intelligent but very careless. I was surprised that he made it to college by doing work that an elementary student could do. Unfortunately, when my father snapped out of his bad habits, it was too late for him to get a decent job. His siblings were either successful or married someone from the middle class, and since my grandfather died, the only person who could support him if he failed college, my father had no choice but to take over my grandfather's restaurant. I know he could've gotten a decent job if he actually tried his best.

Although it seemed that he was stuck with the restaurant, he went back to his old, ridiculous self until I came into his dull life. My biological mother wasn't actually married to my father, so I had a different last name back then until my father married my stepmother and finally changed it.

My mother left me with my father when I was born. My father felt like he really had no meaning in life until I was born. He miraculously changed and quit smoking and drinking. Although he was trying his best to be a good role model, we were still living in a situation that no one would want. My caring father tried his best to make me happy and live a decent life. It didn't really matter to me since I just wanted to meet my real mother back then. The only friend I had was my father who worked day and night. I was a lone wolf until my father met my stepmother.

I still remember the first date they went on because I went with them along with her niece.

"Unsa man ang ngalan nimo?" my stepmother said while giving me a normal face.

"AJ," I replied shyly, but I was lucky that it was the only question she asked me that whole night. My father wasn't really a great teacher, so I would talk to people without them understanding what I meant.

They eventually got married and I finally found out that she was a pediatrician. I became close friends with her niece and finally got to live in a house since my father and I lived in that old and dusty restaurant until that point.

The rest of the two weeks in California before we departed to New York were fun and I thought that I should be grateful for my life because I could have sill been living in state that no one deserves to live in.